CLIMBING YOUR FAMILY TREE

By Timothy Keesee

 BOB JONES UNIVERSITY PR
Greenville, South Carolina 29614

NOTE:
The fact that materials produced by other publishers are referred to in this volume does not constitute an endorsement by Bob Jones University Press of the content or theological position of materials produced by such publishers. The position of Bob Jones University Press, and the University itself, is well known. Any references and ancillary materials are listed as an aid to the reader and in an attempt to maintain the accepted academic standards of the publishing industry.

Climbing Your Family Tree

Timothy Keesee, Ed.D.

Editor: Brenda Thompson Schoolfield

Cover: Roger Bruckner

Photo Credits:
Cover: Unusual Films
Laurie K. Bopp: 40 (bottom)
Timothy Keesee: 40 (top, middle), 41 (all)

©1992 Bob Jones University Press
Greenville, South Carolina 29614

Printed in the United States of America

ISBN 0-89084-611-1

20   19   18   17   16   15   14   13   12   11   10   9   8   7   6

To the Memory of my Grandfather
William Henry Keesee
and our pursuit of the past

Contents

1
Portraits

My clue, my only clue, had been faded by seventy winters. My grandmother's gray memory of a funeral she had attended as a young girl had led me one fall day to a rolling Virginia woodland in search of my great-great-great-grandmother.

I had long admired Margaret Oakes, my distant matron. Her husband had marched off to war in the spring of 1862 only to be cut down at a sleepy little crossroads called Gettysburg in an immortal assault known as Pickett's Charge. Bereft with a brood of six in her care, she kept the family together and kept the farm going. From all accounts, the hard times that descended on the land more than met their match in Widow Margaret. After thrashing through the woods and brambles for some time, I was at last rewarded. White marble stood out against the autumn carpet.

As I swept back years of neglect, the lichen-covered letters told me my search was over. I could at last pay my respects to this courageous woman. As I walked away from that quiet resting place, I was reminded again of the personal satisfaction that family history research provides, as well as the personal responsibility to share it with the next generation. My children will come to this forgotten place and hear the story of Margaret.

The Blush of Life

A family history is far more than a dry chronicle of names and dates ever receding into the mists of forgottenness. A family history is a *family's* history—a remarkable, personal, unique story of men and women whose lives merged into relations of love and blood and providence. Your role as a genealogist is to be a gatherer and caretaker of their life story, which is by extension the preface to your own life story.

Only time and ignorance create the remoteness that makes our ancestors seem as stiff and monochrome as a fading tintype. But they were as real as you and I—their faces blushed with life. They had homes and headaches and hearty laughter, and they had voices, voices that could tell the most interesting stories. Like the time your great-great-grandfather braved a hail of lead across a little creek called Bull Run, and how later he and his clan survived the Kansas winter of 1883 after losing most of their crop to a prairie fire. And then there was your grandfather, who wasn't always a stooped old man or a distant memory. There was the time he was a little boy with a raging fever. It was 1919, and the Great Influenza epidemic in America had already claimed more lives than the Great War had. His mother feared and prayed and wept and finally saw her son miraculously slip out of the Grim Reaper's grasping hands. And your grandmother—what a lovely bride! She turned down countless suitors before settling on the right man—perhaps it was his shiny, new Model T? And the way she kept four children fed and clothed through the Depression should have easily qualified her for the Nobel Prize in economics.

History Lessons

Besides the human drama of your family's past, there are also lessons behind their lives. First of all, there are lessons about history in general. It is a simple, obvious, and yet profound fact that because we are alive today, we have a direct line of ancestors that have been a part of every era of human history. At times perhaps some were at center stage in the great events of the past; others perhaps occupied a back seat in the balcony, but all had their part. Learning about your personal past will naturally ignite interest in America's past. Whether your ancestors wore blue or gray or both during the Civil War, you will doubtless want to learn about the battles they fought in. If they joined a wagon train heading for Oregon, you will want to read *Women's Diaries of the Westward Journey* to get a feel for the trail. Maybe you found a photograph of your grandmother, and though she would never agree, from all appearances she was a *flapper*. What made the 1920s roar? How did Babe Ruth and Calvin Coolidge, Charles Lindbergh and Mary Pickford make the decade when your grandmother was a young woman the most colorful of the twentieth century?

Simply put, your family's history is a microcosm of history. In revolution and expansion, immigration and industrialization, from the farm to the factory, from sodhouses to the suburbs, your ancestors were history makers who shaped and reflected national trends and great events.

Yet beyond the history lessons are personal lessons. The more we know about our forebears, their struggles and achievements, the more we are fortified to meet our own challenges. Winston Churchill once remarked, "We have not journeyed all this way across the centuries, across the oceans, across the mountains, across the prairies, because we are made of sugar candy." The lessons from life that a family's history provides are perhaps not always the stuff of headlines; they are bigger than that—lessons written with blood, sweat, and tears. When I read Jefferson's Declaration, "We mutually pledge to each other our lives, our fortunes, and our sacred honor," I am stirred with pride to know that *my* people helped seal that pledge in battle, that the defense of liberty is a personal, not simply a political, heritage. And when, for example, I struggle with the demands of parenting, I am both challenged and encouraged by grandparents who raised twelve children and who in the twilight of life could smile back upon sixty-seven springtimes together.

Tempus Fugit

As you climb your family tree you will naturally want to shake as many of its branches as possible, and perhaps if sturdy enough, they may invite further climbing. As you climb, however, one overarching consideration to keep in mind may be summed up with the simple Latin phrase that adorns the face of old clocks—*Tempus Fugit*—time is flying. A family's history exists not only in the bones of a distant past but also in the flesh and blood of the present. Yet it is a present ever slipping into the past. Twenty years ago I sat by a hearth in a Virginia farmhouse and asked my grandfather Keesee questions about his past. He told his stories of war and peace, of happy times and hard times. Now his voice has been silenced by time; the house where we sat, since abandoned, sadly has slumped into disrepair. Yet I have recorded his memories, and they live through me. My children and their children too shall have them and know them. Every family has its origins, stories, and traditions, which, collected before they slip away, become an heirloom for tomorrow that each generation may enjoy and pass along with their own additions. Such an heirloom, priceless and personal, gathered from lichened marble, yellow parchment, and old friends, offers intimate portraits from the album of life.

2
What's in a Name?

As you climb your family tree to its distant branches, one of the remarkable discoveries that awaits you is the number and diversity of lineages that flow together like streams in confluence to form your family. Consider, for example, that during a period of only ten generations, or roughly since the days of George Washington, every person has 1,022 direct ancestors drawn from over 500 different family lines. This accumulation of surnames represents keys to your past. So the answer to Shakespeare's well-worn question "What's in a name?" may be Danish and English, Russian and Prussian, Turkish and Yiddish. The rich diversity of names of families drawn to these shores from many lands is part of your heritage. As the building blocks of your genealogy, names warrant close study.

Surnames

Before the twelfth century most people did not have surnames. For people living in the scattered rural isolation of medieval times, last names were not necessary. By the early Renaissance, however, with the rise of towns and the growth in population, surnames became increasingly common. Interestingly, in a 1465 decree King Edward V ordered his Irish subjects to adopt surnames "either of some town, or some colour, as Blacke or Brown, or some Art or Science, as Smyth or Carpenter, or some office as Cooke or Butler.''

This edict underscores the origin of many last names. Surnames were often derived from three simple sources: what a person did, where he lived, or who his father was.

Occupational—Occupations commonly served as surnames, particularly in a day in which a trade was a family affair with work skills passed down like heirlooms from one generation to the next. In every town certain names told not only who a man was but what he was as well. John Smith owned a forge. William Baker made bread. Robert Tailor was handy with a needle and thread, and Thomas Cooper made barrels for the man who ground wheat for Bill Baker's bread shop—a Mr. Miller, of course.

Occupational names of English origin are rather easy to spot, though some such as Chandler, a candle-maker, and Sherman, a man skilled with shearing sheep or working cloth require a little imagination. Non-English surnames, however, require some knowledge of the native tongue. Keesee, for example, is derived from the German word *käse,* ''cheese,'' making Keesee an occupational surname for ''cheese maker.''

This overview of occupational surnames and a look at other types to follow should dispel one common myth about family origins—that everyone with the same last name derives from a common ancestor. There were many German cheesemakers, as there were many English butchers, bakers, and candlestick makers. Only the most unusual surnames could possibly issue from a single source. Even then the researcher must be careful to recognize that some uncommon names are simply uncommon spellings of common names.

Geographic—Where a person resided also provided a source for surnames. Names such as Hill, Meadows, Rivers, and Wood have obvious derivations. At times prepositions provided prefixes for geographic surnames; for example,

Atte Water (a surname for one who lived by a body of water) became Atwater. Atte Lea (by a meadow) became Attlee, Atleigh, or just Lee. The French *de* for *of* still survives in surnames such as Deloach and Devine.

Patronymic—The name of the head of a family or clan also provided a common source for surnames. Johnson, son of John; Robertson, son of Robert; Gibson, son of Gib or Gilbert are but a few examples of English patronymic surnames. Other national origins provide their own paternal designations. The suffix *sen* is Danish for "son of" as is the Scottish prefix *Mac* or *Mc*, the Norman *Fitz*, and the Irish *O'*. Some patronymic surnames have been condensed or corrupted over time, making them more difficult to identify. For example, in Welsh "son of" is designated by the prefix *Ap*. Ap Howell, "son of Howell," has come down to us as "Powell."

Spellings and Mispelingz

Everyone likes to think that the spelling of his last name is the "correct" spelling that has bravely weathered the centuries in its present form. Sooner or later, however, the family historian is likely to find that things are not always so tidy. The problem of spelling variations is caused by two main culprits: anglicization and inaccurate records. Many non-English immigrants, particularly during the colonial and early national period, changed the spelling of their names to fit into the language and culture of their adopted land. Sometimes this change involved a simple translation, such as the German Schwartz to "Black" or Weiss to "White." More commonly, however, Weiss would be anglicized to "Wise." The French Huguenot Apollos Rivoire came to Boston in the 1730s and decided to remove one of the impediments he felt to joining the ranks of the merchant class. In his own words, "merely on account that the bumpkins pronounce it easier," he changed his name to Paul

Climbing Your Family Tree

Revere. His son, Paul, Jr., became the famous midnight rider and hero of the American Revolution.

Perhaps the most common and sometimes the most puzzling source of spelling variation comes from inaccurate records. Careless or unskilled clerks may simply have spelled a name as they heard it. If your ancestor was unlettered, as many of ours were, he would have no way of setting the record straight. Or, if he could write, perhaps he was a poor speller himself and spelled his name phonetically or worse and then passed his creation on to his descendants.

Given the state of record keeping in early America, it is not unusual to find even brothers spelling their last names differently. One man might spell his surname ''Gibson'' while his brother would spell it ''Gipson.'' As Figure 2-1 indicates, the Berkstresser family underwent three spelling changes in as many generations, besides the clerical variations. Sometimes what may seem like a different lineage altogether may just be a different branch on the same old family tree.

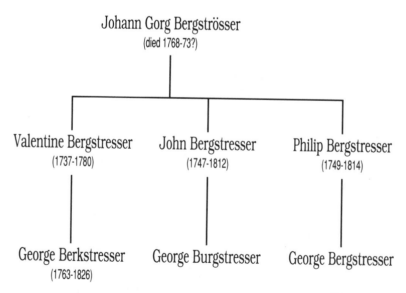

Johann Gorg Bergströsser
(died 1768-73?)

Valentine Bergstresser
(1737-1780)

John Bergstresser
(1747-1812)

Philip Bergstresser
(1749-1814)

George Berkstresser
(1763-1826)

George Burgstresser

George Bergstresser

Figure 2-1   *Surname spellings of the Berkstresser family*

Spelling variations are a problem particularly in tracing census records. Regarding many of the early census-takers, we can only hope that they could count better than they could spell. The 1790 census, for example, contains thirty-four variations on the name ''Reynolds,'' including such notorious attempts as ''Ranals'' and ''Rinnolds.'' We shall take a closer look at how to make sense of the census in Chapter 6.

Naturally, first names are just as subject to spelling variations as last names. But first names are also subject to an additional problem—deciphering nicknames. This is particularly true when your only information comes from interviews with relatives, old letters, or the family Bible. Amy, for example, may stand for ''Amanda,'' or it may stand for ''America,'' a name some patriotic fathers bequeathed to their daughters a century ago. My father had an aunt whom he knew only as ''Aunt Pokey.'' That name always seemed to me to be rather unflattering until I came across her grave some time ago and found that her name was really Pocahontas—a distinguished Virginia name.

Knights and Names

One area of name study that merits mention at this point is heraldry. Coats of arms as we know them today originated about the eleventh century, about the time of the Crusades. Evidently during those chivalric days if you saw one knight in shining armor, you had seen them all. Therefore, knights wore distinctive tunics, or ''coats,'' embroidered with symbols of Scriptural or martial significance, and they fixed such symbols on their shields. Sir Walter Scott, in his classic *Ivanhoe,* captured the day when heraldic emblems were badges of battle, and lances and lion-hearted men ruled the fields of honor:

His suit of armour was formed of steel, richly inlaid with gold, and the device on his shield was a young oak-

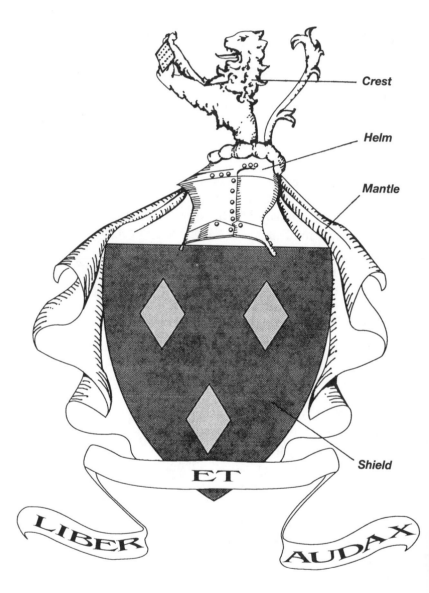

Crest

Helm

Mantle

Shield

Motto *"Free and Bold"*

Figure 2-2 *Coat of arms for the Freeman family*

tree pulled up by the roots, with the Spanish word *Des-dichado,* signifying Disinherited. He was mounted on a gallant black horse, and as he passed through the lists he gracefully saluted the Prince and the ladies by lowering his lance. . . . He then commanded his trumpet to sound a defiance to the challengers, and desired a herald to announce to them that he should make no election, but was willing to encounter them in the order in which they pleased to advance against him. The gigantic Front-de-Bœuf, armed in sable armour, was the first who took the field. He bore on a white shield a black bull's head, half defaced by the numerous encounters which he had undergone, and bearing the arrogant motto. *Cave, Adsum* ["Beware I am Here"]

In Coleridge's words, *"The knights are dust. And their good swords are rust."* It might be added, however, that their coats of arms have survived quite well. Because of the general illiteracy of the age (from the sixth to the eleventh century, for example, only three English kings could sign their own names), coats of arms passed along to succeeding generations and became a kind of pictorial autograph fashioned into seals for use on family correspondence. Since these armorial images could be forged or similar designs mistaken for each other, in the sixteenth century, coats of arms were chronicled and registered. These records naturally provide the authentication for coats of arms today.

Having such a badge of distinction was, of course, desirable for prestige and position. Yet if one were not "to the manor borne," what was a commoner to do? Be creative. Many heraldic devices were not drawn up on the Round Table; they were created by the merchant class of the late Renaissance who had the money but not the blood of nobility. Because they craved status symbols, it was only natural that they would create and register their own coats of arms, which only underscores the fact that not all coats of arms were created equal. To possess one is not necessarily to possess an attribution of nobility.

With the exception of a run-in with George III a couple of centuries ago, Americans have a long-standing infatuation with European royalty and nobility. Often as a result, coats of arms are sought for the Old World link they provide. Be cautious, however, when offered coats of arms from commercial researchers, particularly those who seem more interested in the ''commerce'' than the ''research.'' Clear documentation should always be provided if the offer and the company are legitimate. In addition, keep in mind that since the same surnames do not always issue from a common ancestor, simply discovering a coat of arms with your name on it does not necessarily mean it came from your lineage.

If you can lay documented claim to a coat of arms, it will naturally make a colorful addition to your family history. If you can't, do not be concerned. Whether of low or high birth, your ancestors who sought these shores, braved the wilderness, trekked the trackless prairie, and from every land became ''this new man, this American'' have their own badges of distinction written in life and the land. As a genealogist, it is your responsibility—and your privilege—to learn and tell their story.

3
Organizing
Your History

A genealogist must be not only a diligent detective uncovering the people and places of his past but also a conscientious record keeper. You can use any number of methods to organize your family history; the important thing, however, is to have a method. A poorly organized history is like a puzzle with missing pieces. Valuable information is inevitably lost, sometimes irretrievably so.

The Three Rs

A family history can be divided into three broad categories: Register, Records, and Reminiscences. Three-ring binders are perhaps best suited for such divisions because you can add pages easily. You may also find it helpful to begin with two binders, a volume for your father's side and one for your mother's.

Names, residences, and dates—of birth, death, and marriage—compose a basic family *Register*. It is important that you *begin with yourself* and work backward. Working forward from a name in the past will often waste a lot of time with little or nothing to show for it. It is best if your family register is chronicled in chart form, which will simplify and standardize your information. We will look at some helpful chart formats later in this chapter.

Climbing Your Family Tree

The *Records* section of your genealogy should include photocopies of marriage and birth certificates, as well as family photographs, postcards, excerpts from old diaries and letters, autographs, newspaper clippings about family members, and even recipes. These materials, carefully documented and preserved, will add foliage to the bare branches of your family tree outlined in the Register.

The *Reminiscences* category is the human dimension of your history, preserving the anecdotes and incidents of family life. Despite its importance, it is the area most often overlooked and most easily lost. Sometimes in our acquisitive drive to collect all of our ancestors of long ago and far away we forget about our relatives that are here today and perhaps gone tomorrow. The amusing story about how your grandparents eloped or the dramatic account about how your uncle and some other GIs faced a German patrol in a bloody shootout in the fall of '44 will mean more to you than finding out the names of all of your great-great-great-grandparents' children. Such information can and should be tracked down from a will or census schedule or a tombstone, but over time memories are far less durable than paper and stone.

If you can draw from the memories of older relatives, it is possible to bring even a century-old incident to the surface and capture it in print. Recently my grandfather Jones recalled an incident he had heard about his grandfather's Civil War experiences. The old Confederate, though losing an arm to a Yankee bullet, said there was one thing in particular he regretted from the war. Despite all the bloodshed he had witnessed, experienced, and even caused, the event that the gray warrior most wistfully remembered was that once in the desperation of near starvation he and his comrades had "requisitioned" an old woman's pig and eaten it. This old story, so touched with irony and humanness, is part of no official military record; it is a captured memory from a very long time ago. As a family historian, you must gather not only the past but also the present and perpetuate your family memories.

One caution, however, when recording Reminiscences is to keep your eyes and ears open to myths and legends that have crept into the family story. Reminiscences should be more a product of a vivid memory than a vivid imagination. If, for example, because your surname is Jackson and your family migrated from Tennessee, the story has circulated that you are descended from "Old Hickory," President Andrew Jackson, do some checking before recording this story as history. Since Jackson never had any children, the case for descent is rather unlikely. It is not that the old timers are intentionally lying, it's just that over time an embellished story or a wild conjecture takes on a life of its own. It *seems* to be true because, like an heirloom, it has been passed down from one generation to the next. And also like an heirloom, no matter how tattered by facts a story may be, it is difficult to part with.

Do not be cynical about family stories, but do be cautious. Whenever you can, see whether they square with other information you have gathered. For years my grandmother told me that her great-grandfather who fought under the command of Stonewall Jackson was wounded in battle. After his wife nursed him back to health, he returned to his old regiment only to die at the very end of the war. The story concerned me somewhat, for though I had a number of the old warrior's letters, there was no indication he had ever been wounded in battle—until I tracked down his official service record in the National Archives. He had indeed been wounded at Cedar Mountain, had rejoined, and then died about the time of Appomattox. The story passed by word of mouth across five generations had proven accurate, but this is not always the case. Enjoy your family lore, but always keep a discerning eye out for the line between fact and fiction.

Charting Your Past

The simplest format for gathering basic genealogical information for the Register of names and dates is the Five-Generation Chart (5-G). Figure 3-1 illustrates a 5-G which includes the vital records of birth, marriage, residence, and death, if known. Obviously, lack of space at certain points prohibits the inclusion of other important information such as the names of brothers and sisters, birthplaces, or location of burial. This information is handled on a different form, the Family Data Sheet, which we will examine separately.

Notice that the 5-G Chart illustrated is lettered A, with each entry numbered. The letter and number will be used to reference subsequent charts and Family Data Sheets. Any entry on Chart A can be the first entry in subsequent charts, but the name will continue to carry its initial letter/number designation. As Figure 3-2 indicates, Chart B takes up the entry of *William Henry Keesee,* reference A/8, and traces back from there. If a 5-G Chart were compiled for the entry of *Stephen Murphy*, that name would be number 1 on such a chart, but the reference would be B/18 since that is the initial entry for that name.

There are several things to observe about the information included on the 5-G Chart. First of all, the letters *b*, *m*, and *d* are used to designate dates of birth, marriage, and death respectively. The letter *c* stands for *circa,* Latin for "about," and may be used where precise dates are as yet unknown. Children's names may be included as space permits. In addition, list all maternal entries using their maiden names.

Five-Generation Charts provide the simplest means to organize and conceptualize a genealogy. They also make spotting areas that need work easy. If you are just starting out, this may not seem like a problem, but as knowledge of your family tree grows, gaps and question marks will increase as well. That is not hard to imagine when you consider you have sixteen great-great-grandparents—a number that of course *quadruples* to sixty-four just two generations further back!

The 5-G Chart provides the framework for the "house" of your family history; the Family Data Sheet (FDS) will help provide a better picture of the occupants of this house. As the name implies, the Family Data Sheet is oriented to a particular family with space available for information about a couple's offspring. Typically, as Figure 3-3 indicates, the FDS is labeled with the head of the household's name and referenced to that individual's initial 5-G Chart entry code. In this example, Jesse Keesee can be found on Chart B, number 8. Whenever possible, locations of birthplaces, residences, or grave sites should be written down, including approximate distances, road numbers, or street addresses. Of course *you* know where grandpa's old farmhouse stands and the churchyard where he is buried, but a generation or so from now your descendants will probably not know unless you write it down.

The Family Data Sheet is one of the genealogist's most useful organizing tools. You may want to keep them together as a group following the Five-Generation Charts in the Register Section of your family history notebook and perhaps include a copy of select Family Data Sheets to introduce a photograph or autograph collection from the members of that particular family.

Now that you have two basic forms for organizing your genealogy, it is time to take a detailed look at methods for filling in those blank spaces. This is, in fact, the best part of a family historian's work—the search for ancestors. It is an adventure that will take you all the way from crumbling tombstones to computer terminals and from musty archives to Mom's kitchen for coffee and conversation about the way things used to be.

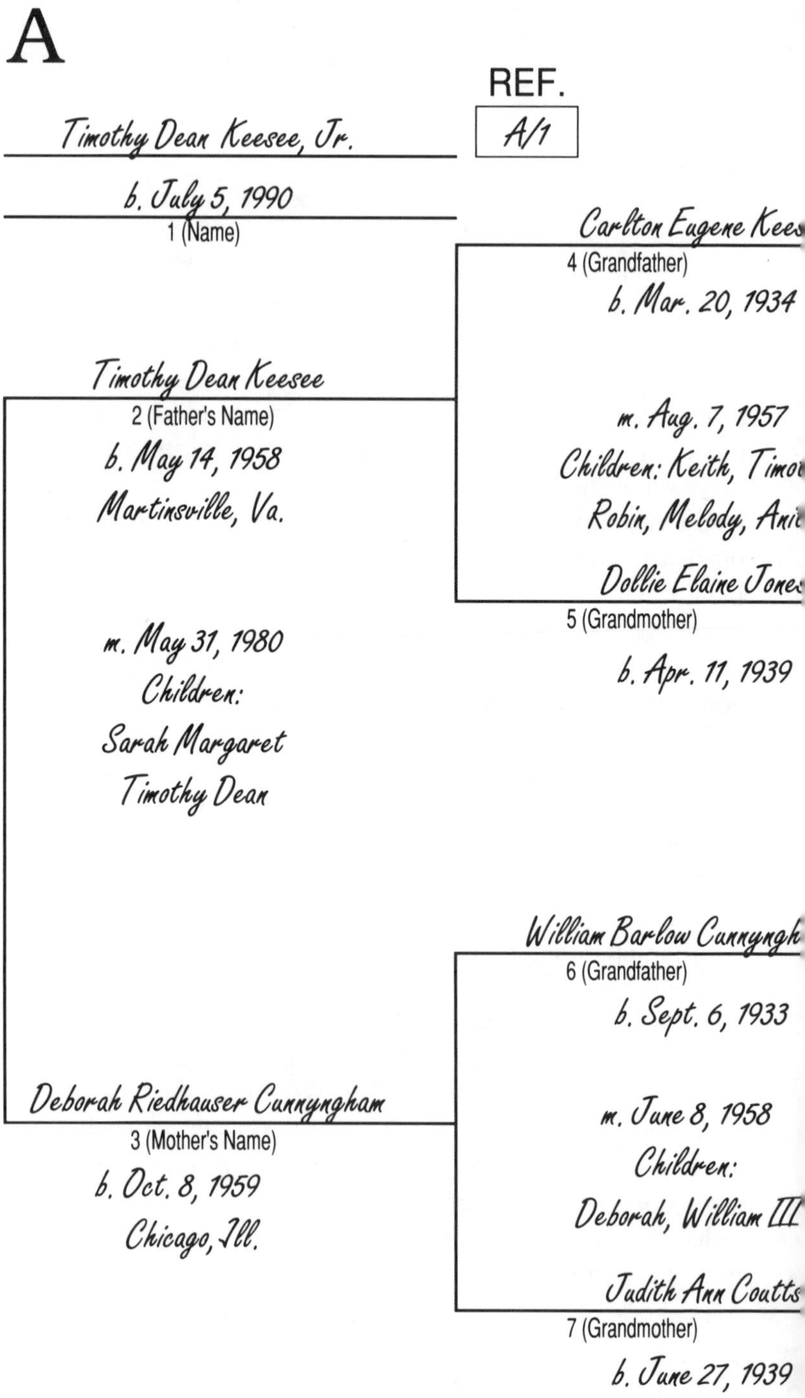

A

Timothy Dean Keesee, Jr.

b. July 5, 1990
1 (Name)

Carlton Eugene Kees
4 (Grandfather)
b. Mar. 20, 1934

Timothy Dean Keesee
2 (Father's Name)
b. May 14, 1958
Martinsville, Va.

m. Aug. 7, 1957
Children: Keith, Timo
Robin, Melody, Ani

Dollie Elaine Jones
5 (Grandmother)
b. Apr. 11, 1939

m. May 31, 1980
Children:
Sarah Margaret
Timothy Dean

William Barlow Cunnyngh
6 (Grandfather)
b. Sept. 6, 1933

m. June 8, 1958
Children:
Deborah, William III

Deborah Riedhauser Cunnyngham
3 (Mother's Name)
b. Oct. 8, 1959
Chicago, Ill.

Judith Ann Coutts
7 (Grandmother)
b. June 27, 1939

Figure 3-1 *5-G chart of Timothy Dean Keesee, Jr.*

	John Thomas Keesee
William Henry Keesee	16 (Great-Great-Grandfather)
8 (Great-Grandfather)	*m. Dec. 25, 1898*
	Lula Belle Burnett
m. Feb. 28, 1933	17 (Great-Great-Grandmother)
	William Gibson
Abrie Gillie Gibson	18 (Great-Great-Grandfather)
9 (Great-Grandmother)	*m. Nov. 4, 1902*
	Palitica Ella Oakes
	19 (Great-Great-Grandmother)
	James Edward Jones
Leonard Frank Jones	20 (Great-Great-Grandfather)
10 (Great-Grandfather)	*m. Dec. 25, 1899*
	Mary Anna Willis
m. Nov. 3, 1923	21 (Great-Great-Grandmother)
	Willie Walter Stowe
Jessie Lou Stowe	22 (Great-Great-Grandfather)
11 (Great-Grandmother)	*m. April 5, 1900*
	Lorena Belle Hearp
	23 (Great-Great-Grandmother)
	Victor Cunnyngham
B. Cunnyngham, Sr.	24 (Great-Great-Grandfather)
12 (Great-Grandfather)	**Nina Barlow**
m. June 11, 1932	25 (Great-Great-Grandmother)
	Harry Smith
Emily Randolph Smith	26 (Great-Great-Grandfather)
13 (Great-Grandmother)	**Stella Satterwaith**
	27 (Great-Great-Grandmother)
	George Coutts
Melvin Toll Coutts	28 (Great-Great-Grandfather)
14 (Great-Grandfather)	*m. June 21, 1904*
	Elsie P. Toll
m. June 26, 1929	29 (Great-Great-Grandmother)
	George Riedhauser
Margaret Lydia Riedhauser	30 (Great-Great-Grandfather)
15 (Great-Grandmother)	*m. June 15, 1904*
	Minnie Mattull
	31 (Great-Great-Grandmother)

19

B

William Henry Keesee

b. Aug. 24, 1905 Smith Mountain, Va.
1 (Name)
d. March 12, 1978 Callands, Va.

Walter Nangle Kee
4 (Grandfather)
b. 1856
d. 1928
m. Jan. 21, 1875

John Thomas Keesee
2 (Father's Name)
b. 1878
d. ?

m. Dec. 25, 1898
Children:
Essie Lee Keesee
(Matherly)
1902-1934
William Henry

Virginia J. Marti.
5 (Grandmother)
b. 1857
d. 1931

John W. Burnet.
6 (Grandfather)
b. 1843
Pittsylvania County,
m. Dec. 25, 1873

Lula Belle Burnett
3 (Mother's Name)
b. c. 1884
d. July 5, 1960
buried Museville, Va.
near Turkey Cock Mtn.

Susan A. Barber
7 (Grandmother)
b. 1851
Franklin County, V

20   **Figure 3-2** *5-G chart of William Henry Keesee*

Jesse Keesee
8 (Great-Grandfather)
m. Dec. 21, 1846

Booker Keesee
16 (Great-Great-Grandfather)
m. Feb. 21, 1814
Jane Dove
17 (Great-Great-Grandmother)

Louisa Murphy
9 (Great-Grandmother)

Stephen Murphy
18 (Great-Great-Grandfather)
m. Dec. 4, 1820
Lucy Baber
19 (Great-Great-Grandmother)

John Martin
10 (Great-Grandfather)

20 (Great-Great-Grandfather)

21 (Great-Great-Grandmother)

Harriett (?)
11 (Great-Grandmother)

22 (Great-Great-Grandfather)

23 (Great-Great-Grandmother)

James Burnett
12 (Great-Grandfather)
m. Aug. 2, 1825

John Burnett ?
24 (Great-Great-Grandfather)
m. Mar. 13, 1792
Judith Becke
25 (Great-Great-Grandmother)

Rebecca Nicholas
13 (Great-Grandmother)

Charles Nicholas
26 (Great-Great-Grandfather)
m. Sept. 6, 1786
Marshall Farthing
27 (Great-Great-Grandmother)

Gustin L. Barber
14 (Great-Grandfather)

28 (Great-Great-Grandfather)

29 (Great-Great-Grandmother)

Elizabeth M. (?)
15 (Great-Grandmother)

30 (Great-Great-Grandfather)

31 (Great-Great-Grandmother)

21

FAMILY DATA SHEET

Jesse Keesee Family		

Name of husband: Jesse Keesee   REF. *B/8*

Birth date: *July 22, 18*
Birthplace: *Pittsylvania*
Death date: *Nov. 19, 18*
Burial place: *Near Gre*
intersection Rds.

Name of wife (maiden name): Louisa Murphy   REF. *B/9*

Birth date: *April 25, 182*
Birthplace: *Pittsylvania C*
Death date: *Nov. 5, 190*
Burial place: *same as U*

Marriage date: *Dec. 21, 1846*
Place: *Pittsylvania County, Va.*

Other spouses:

#	Sex	Children	Birth	Death	Married to
1	M	Thomas Lynch	1849	?	Sally ?
2	M	Stephen Booker	?	1914	Martha Tuck
3	M	Robert William	1853	?	Virginia Mayhue
4	F	Walter Nangle	1856	1928	Virginia Martin
5	M	Melissa Ann	?	?	Thomas Crouch
6	M	Alonzo Buchanon	1858	1945	Sally H. Hardy
7	F	Harriet Margaret	?	?	unmarried
8	F	Lucy Jane	1861	1943	David Mayhue
9					
10					
11					
12					

Additional Notes Husband: *Occupation: Miller at a grist mill on Old Woman's Creek near Sycamore.*

Parents: *Booker Keesee / Jane Dove*

Wife: *Louisia's father was a veteran of the War of 1812.*

Parents: *Stephen Murphy 1793 / Lucy Baber 1796–?*

4
Family Sources

Generally the most immediate sources for family history information are you and your family. Your relatives, particularly older ones, are among your most valuable resources. Often they can extend your family tree back two or three more generations by memory alone. In addition, family members can provide information that is difficult or impossible to learn from public sources. This does not mean that all of your relatives will be knowledgeable, lucid, or even cooperative. With some planning and persistence, however, you should be able to get even the most confirmed curmudgeon of the family to contribute something to the genealogy. Let us take a closer look at some of the ways to gather important information from your kin.

Face to Face

Interviewing relatives is often the best place to start gathering genealogical information. The two most important things to keep in mind are to plan your questions in advance and to chronicle carefully the information afterwards from your notes or recordings. Other suggestions for successful interviews follow.

First Things First—Be sure to gather all the information you can from the interviewee to fill in blanks on your Five-Generation Charts and Family Data Sheets. Asking your relative is often the easiest and sometimes only way to learn full names of children, birth and death dates, and residences. It may be helpful to take a 5-G Chart or FDS along with you and jot down pertinent information right on the form. Later you can recopy it in a neater hand.

Scripts and Scribble—To begin with, have your questions in hand while conducting the interview. This, of course, does not mean you cannot depart from the script; it does mean you will have some direction and key talking points. This is particularly important if you are conducting an interview over the telephone. A spiral notebook is usually best for taking notes in, but be sure to record the date of the interview and recopy the information later on a separate interview form, particularly if your scrawl tends to cool into illegibility.

Audio/Visuals—In some cases you may want to tape record or videotape the interview. For taping that special interview, such as Grandpa recounting his war stories or an aunt telling tales of mischief and mayhem about your dad, always use the best quality tapes. If recording with a VCR, set the camera on a tripod and use the fastest recording speed to permit enhanced duplication. Of course, a sense of awkwardness usually comes when recording equipment is invited into a conversation; try to create as relaxed an atmosphere as possible by focusing on the interviewee rather than the equipment. If there is genuine resistance to having the conversation recorded, naturally you should respect that wish. Do not allow insistence on a particular method of gathering information to keep you from actually getting that information. The atmosphere of any interview should not be that of a documentary; it should be that of a family enjoying each other's company.

Time to Talk—Timing *is* everything when it comes to interviewing relatives. Try to conduct the interview when you have *time* to talk. This may not necessarily include family reunions or funeral gatherings. Whether it is a rainy Sunday afternoon or an evening set aside during a family vacation back home, try to find a time in which distractions can be kept to a minimum.

Second Round—You will often take away more questions from an interview, particularly after reflection. Subsequent interviews can help answer new questions and verify old answers. As we all know from experience, memories are not always reliable. In a second interview it is often useful to ask some of the same questions again. Be careful, however, not to "lead the witness" with your questioning. For example, do not say, "Granddad, you have said that your brother Gilbert died in the winter of 1914 when you were nine years old. What did he die from?" It would perhaps be better to ask, "Tell me about your brother who died when you were young." If a discrepancy in dates, names, or circumstances crops up, you can tactfully ask for clarification. Oftentimes, critical problems can be resolved or colorful details added in a carefully considered follow-up interview.

Careful Questions—Though memories can be a source of joy and strength, they can also be a source of great pain. It is easy in an interview to be so concerned about compiling a genealogy that we are insensitive to the emotions that our questions can revive. This was brought home to me years ago when I first began recording my family's history. I had been asking my grandmother questions about the baby boy she had lost to pneumonia forty years earlier. She gave me his name and dates, but there seemed to be something missing in her voice. Later she took out an old box. Her son had been taken in the early spring of 1934—the box contained an Easter basket the child had been too sick to enjoy, brown crumbling flowers from his grave, and a little shirt yellowed by time and perhaps tears. Now some people may have shrugged at such a pitiful, morbid, little collection as if it too should have been buried long ago. But I think to my grandmother, in memory, those lilies were still fresh and fragrant, the battered old basket was bright green, filled with fresh chocolates that a young mother had sacrificed to buy in order to brighten her baby's last dim, feverish days. I quietly watched all of this; I wanted to know more about her son. But I dared not intrude further on her thoughts— and yet as I reflected, she had already taught me much, for without words she had lifted the curtain on a mother's enduring love. As you talk with relatives, be sensitive to their emotions, for the ancestor that to you may be only a blank on a 5-G Chart was to them perhaps a cherished loved one and friend.

Thus far we have considered the style of an interview, but what of its substance? To begin with, stretch your relatives' memories as far back as they will take you to add information to the Register. This will often provide crucial leads for your search through official sources. In addition, it is interesting to learn from your older relatives about their participation in or reaction to great national events. What was it like growing up during the Great Depression? Where were they when the news first broke that the Japanese had attacked Pearl Harbor or that the president had been gunned down in Dallas? Who was the first candidate for president they ever voted for and why? Who was the most famous person they ever met? Perhaps, like my grandfather, they saw Charles Lindbergh barnstorming or in a chance encounter snapped a salute to that indomitable giant of the century, Winston Churchill. Answers to such questions will give the pages of a history book a fresh, personal appeal.

Besides the ''history'' questions, do not overlook the personal ones; from these you will often come away with some delightful stories. What was their worst day in school? Who was their favorite teacher and why? What kind of car did they first drive? How did they first meet that special someone they eventually married? What is their favorite hymn? Where have they lived and where have they traveled? Answers to some of these questions may be included on the

Family Data Sheet. Perhaps it is best, because of space restraints in the FDS, to write up the stories of courtship and combat, of humor and hardship in a full narrative form, appropriately referenced and included in the Reminiscences section of your family history.

Corresponding Kin

Letters are another important means of gathering genealogical and anecdotal information. Letter writing is particularly useful if you need to focus on only a few questions. Letters also provide something special that no other medium can—a personal souvenir of the person's handwriting in which his thoughts and memories are set down on paper.

If your pen pal turns out to be a reluctant writer, you might want to make your request as easy on him as possible. As Figure 4-1 illustrates, typed questions with space provided to write in the answer may make letter writing a little less formidable. This approach has its advantages, chief of which is that you are likely to get an answer to most of your questions, even if the answer is "I don't know." The major drawbacks, however, are that forms tend to remove some of the intimacy and immediacy from the correspondence, and if adequate space is not provided, an inadequate answer may be given. In short, provide your letter writer with as much freedom as possible to express himself, and results will often be a full, lively account.

Here are some questions that may be used in an interview or on a questionnaire.

1. How did you meet your spouse?
2. Where did you attend school and for how long?
3. What was your favorite subject in school?
4. What was your least favorite subject in school?
5. Describe the teacher who influenced you the most.
6. Did you have a favorite pet?
7. What was the first car you drove?

Family Q & A

Full name:	REF.
Leonard Frank Jones	*A/10*

Subject:

Early Life

___*December 12, 1904*___   ___*Flint Hill Pittsylvania County, Va.*___
Birth date   Birth place

1. What do you remember about your mother?

She had black hair and I was always told she could sing well. My only real memory of her was of walking behind the 2 horse wagon that carried her coffin to burial. I was 6 years old. She died of tuberculosis.

2. Where did you attend school?

Arlington School near Dry Fork on the old Irish Road. The little schoolhouse has long ago fallen in. I went through the sixth grade. Back then there were only eight grades.

3. Describe your early work experience.

As long as I can remember I worked in the fields. When I was 16 I worked for Richmond Cedar Works. Then I joined the U.S. Army. I was at Fort Monroe, Va. for over 6 months, Dec. 28, 1920 to July 28, 1921—that is when they found out I was only 16 and put me on a train for home. My soldiering days were over.

4. Describe your wedding day.

Your Grandma and I were married at the parsonage of the Whitmell Methodist Church. That was in 1923 and I was driving a brand new Model T. We lived first at Pleasant Gap at Mr. Stowe's and then moved to Danville.

Figure 4-1 *Sample interview letter*

8. Describe the physical appearance and personality of parents, grandparents, and even great-grandparents if possible.
9. What are some of the most enjoyable and influential books you have ever read?
10. Who was the most famous person you have ever met or seen?
11. Who was the first candidate for president you voted for?
12. Describe early jobs that you held.
13. Did you ever serve in the military? When? Where?
14. Describe some of your memorable travels.
15. What is your favorite color?
16. What is your favorite flower?
17. Describe your childhood home.
18. Where did you attend church?
19. What are your favorite hymns?
20. How many times have you moved? Where?

This is just a sample of the kind of questions that will generate fascinating stories and clothe your genealogy with personality. If distances preclude an interview, then consider purchasing a blank book and writing questions at the top of the pages. Send the book along to the relative being interviewed and have them ''fill in the blanks.'' If they cooperate, the result will be a treasured memoir.

Memorabilia

The *stuff* of a family's history can also provide, from a variety of sources, clues to the past.

Family Bible—A prized item in many late nineteenth-century homes was a large, heavily ornamented Bible for reading, for display, and for recording the names and memorable dates in the life of a family. Although a family Bible generally provides only a sketchy register, it is often helpful in chronicling full names and information about the deaths of infant children that fading memories can scarcely recall. One caution, however, about the family Bible as a genealogical source is that although the Bible is as it claims to be—an inspired, inerrant, and infallible Book—the family history recorded therein is not. Oftentimes dates of birth, marriage, and death were written down many years after the fact. In addition, if the chronicler possessed only a rough literacy, consistency in spelling names may have been of little concern. A family Bible can be a helpful resource, but the genealogical information should be compared with other sources whenever possible.

Photographs—It has been suggested that photography "imprisons time in a rectangle," and plainly the camera has done more to preserve and popularize the past than anything else since the invention of the printing press. But photography has not only captured the panorama of great events and the portraits of great men but also kept for us the common faces and places of life long ago. The old adage is no less true in terms of your personal past—family pictures are worth a thousand words in that they capture "in a rectangle" the faces, fashions, and fortunes of the past. Because the style and size of a photograph provide a rough means of dating a picture, particularly during the nineteenth century, a quick look at the development of photography should prove helpful.

In the late 1830s Frenchman Louis Daguerre and Englishman William Henry Talbot developed photography independently. The early photographers were part chemist, part artist, and all pioneer. The process, first described by Talbot as "photogenic drawing," was a struggle with salts, silvers, glass, paper, and iron to create a light-sensitive surface upon which images could be fixed permanently. Because of the long exposure times, the first photographs were mainly of still lifes or buildings. Portraits were difficult, for even with the subject sitting in bright sunlight with his face powdered with flour, exposure time still lasted several minutes. Improvements came rapidly in the 1840s, however, and "daguerrian artists" set up shop or roved the country-side. Families of modest means, who could never afford to have portraits painted, could now own whole albums of pictures that were in many ways more realistic than the best portraits.

Yet photography remained the work of photographers, for only professionals had equipment and experience enough for the delicate art of picture taking. By the 1880s, however, two factors had changed the situation; the development of faster shutter speeds made hand-held cameras possible, and the introduction of roll film by George Eastman made photography affordable. Eastman's famous Kodak camera, invented in 1888, was an instant success. Tens of thousands of Americans, including perhaps some of your turn-of-the-century ancestors, made the box camera a ubiquitous part of their family circle, capturing the images of everyday life on inexpensive paper stock.

Again, keep in mind that the size and style of the photographic medium provides a rough date for an unidentified photograph. For example, you may be shown a cabinet-style photograph of a stiffly posed, handlebar-mustachioed gentleman and told that the man is your great-great-grand-father, who you know died in 1861. Based on the style of the photograph alone, you can know that maybe this was his son or his friend, but it certainly was not your great-great-grandfather!

The original *daguerreotype* used a silver-coated copper plate to capture the image. Daguerre and his contemporaries, after some experimentation, used other surfaces such as glass (an ambrotype) and enameled iron (a ferrotype or tintype). These were often packaged in delicately crafted cases. The ambrotype and tintype enjoyed wide popularity in the United States from the 1850s through the 1870s. Although some tintypes date from as late as 1900, after the Civil War, increasing numbers of photographs were printed on paper stock. Paper photographs, first developed by the

Englishman Talbot, were based on the negative process and could therefore be reproduced (unlike the daguerreotype, in which each image is unique). By the late 1860s small paper photographs measuring 2 1/2" × 4" called *carte de visite* (French for "visiting card") became the craze. People could now exchange pictures with friends and family. For families separated by great distances, photographs provided an important link. A larger style 4 1/4" × 6 1/2" paper image known as a cabinet photograph gradually replaced the *carte de visite,* but by 1890 both styles were, for the most part, swept aside by Eastman's remarkable Kodak.

If you have inherited, or at least have access to, a box of old family photographs, you can glean much from them for your genealogy. Begin by organizing and identifying as many of them as possible with the help of older relatives. Even if you are quite familiar with a person in a photograph, those who follow you may not be, so carefully and legibly identify the image on a back corner of the picture. Next, carefully study the picture with a magnifying glass, looking at the clothes, jewelry, automobiles, furniture, houses, and pets all crystallized in time by the wonder of photography.

If you do not actually own a particular family photograph that would be an important addition to the genealogy, you may consider either photographing it using a close-up lens on a 35mm camera or photocopying the picture on a color photocopier. Whether copying black-and-white or color images, the color copier's superior technology retains the shadows and depth of photographs to a remarkable degree, unlike conventional copiers. Also, keep in mind that older family photographs may have been passed down through a line other than your own, so check with great aunts or distant cousins. Perhaps they will be able to help put a face with a name in your genealogy. I have "discovered" two century-old photographs of my great-great-grandparents through distant cousins this way. Because the photographs had parted paths with my line of the family four generations past, these remarkable old images were completely unknown even to my grandparents.

Old Letters—Before Mr. Bell's telephone came along, the simple letter was the most common means of communication between family and friends. If you are fortunate enough to have access to old family letters, they may contain a wealth of genealogical information. Though purely personal concerns expressed in letters are sometimes interesting and other times, from our detached perspective, puzzling, they often contribute little to the genealogical record. However, letters or their postmarks do help fix an ancestor in a particular time and place; this information is important in tracking down information from official sources such as census records. In addition, family correspondence can sometimes reveal religious and political affiliations, identify economic conditions and health problems, and provide narrative records of births and deaths. Though many old letters are as routine as an average telephone call, some letters will provide remarkable glimpses into your family's life long ago.

Whether you own old family letters or have only access to them, make good photocopies and then carefully store the originals in a safe place. The copies may then be included in the Records section of your genealogy. Photocopying helps protect the originals from the inevitable deterioration brought on by handling, permits you to share treasured letters with other family members, and serves as a hedge against potential fire loss. Always avoid using Scotch tape or rubber cement with originals and photocopies because of the potential for acidic damage.

Newsmakers—Other genealogical memorabilia that may be brought to light out of Grandma's trunk or out of those old scrapbooks in the back of the closet are newspaper clippings. As with old correspondence, make good quality photocopies of news articles in order to protect the fragile originals.

Whether it's a news photo of an uncle's basketball team the year they won the state championship or a story about your great-grandma's prize pies at the county fair, newspaper articles can often fill in interesting details about a family member's achievements, interests, and activities. This information should be included with the appropriate Family Data Sheet.

Perhaps there are not many news-breaking, headline-making articles you can track from your family's past; there is, however, one way that most people do get mentioned in the newspapers. Ironically, it is when they are no longer around to read it—the obituary. Obituaries, particularly older ones, are really miniature biographies, rich with personal and genealogical details. For example, the 1899 obituary of W.G.E. Cunnyngham reads in part:

> Dr. W.G.E. Cunnyngham, the oldest son of Rev. Jesse Cunnyngham, who was a contemporary and friend of Bishops McKendree and Soule, was born in Knox County, December 3, 1820. His father moved to Monroe County when he was still a small boy, and the most of his youth was spent on a farm. His educational advantages were limited to a few months each year at the district school, but his father had a well-selected library, and he read the books found there with uncommon diligence. . . .
>
> He was converted at the early age of 12 years and licensed to preach at 22 and was in 1843 admitted on trial into the Holston Conference. Early in his ministry he, together with eleven other young men pledged themselves to accept any service in any land to which the church might call them.
>
> In 1851 while attending a camp-meeting a letter was received by Rev. Thomas K. Catlett, Presiding Elder, stating that the Board of Missions had determined to send Dr. Cunnyngham to China and in May, 1852, he sailed for China and for nine years labored unceasingly, not only doing much missionary work, but he also became a very accomplished scholar in the Chinese classics. . . .

When searching for obituaries that are three or more generations in the past, keep in mind that they are often difficult to locate, if they exist at all. Families living in rural settings even as late as the early 1900s would have thought it strange to notify the newspapers about the passing of a loved one. The funeral business is actually a rather recent development. Death was a personal, family affair, and funerals were a time of sorrow and socializing for the family and friends that remained. "News" about death was generally verbal and communal, not printed and public.

If your ancestors were city-dwellers, however, you may be able to locate their death notices in the archives of the local newspaper if the publication is long established. Your search for urban obituaries may also be helped by official sources. For example, one of many tedious but invaluable tasks that the Works Projects Administration (WPA) undertook under federal sponsorship during the Great Depression was compiling a death index for Chicago for the period 1871 to 1933. This index, as well as others, is now available on microfilm. You may also find Betty M. Jarboe's *Obituaries: A Guide to Sources* a helpful reference. In your search for the earliest family obituaries, however, do not forget to preserve the more recent ones, so that those who take up your work years from now will have an easier time of it.

Making Memories

While gathering genealogical information from family sources, take full advantage of every opportunity. For example, after interviewing a relative or while attending a reunion, collect the autographs of family members. Autographs may be organized by family groups, or collected by generations, going as far back as possible. Some of the older autographs in Figure 4-2 were photocopied from old receipts, cancelled checks, and marriage bonds.

The camera should also be a part of your family history gathering. Family photographs from today are as important to your history as those passed down from yesterday. Be sure to take photographs of those you interview, as well as

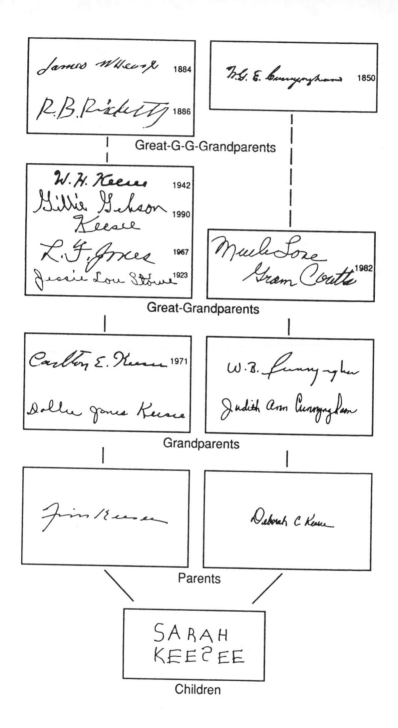

Great-G-G-Grandparents

Great-Grandparents

Grandparents

Parents

Children

Figure 4-2 *Family autograph collection by generation*

pictures of tombstones and houses, particularly birthplaces that you come across in your research. Of course, the best time to think about photographing the important people and places of your family story is while you are researching it, not when it is too late. I recall some years back finding my great-great-grandfather's farmhouse. I did not have a camera with me at the time, but excited over the discovery of this century-old building which had long since passed out of the family's possession, I promised myself I would take a picture the next trip out. A few months later I returned to the site to find only a charred chimney—and a reminder of a lost opportunity to preserve a piece of my family's past.

Family sources provide the foundation for all the genealogical research that follows. From interviews and letter writing to the family photo album, there are many ways to obtain information from your relatives. Yet, as we shall see, more history can be gathered from other family sources—not among the living, but among the dead.

5
Among the Tombs

Gnarled fingers hung down to greet me. The long arms of an ancient oak cast their twisted shadows across the dense underbrush. Briars tugged at my legs, demanding immediate attention. It's not easy finding a dead man.

Following a slim lead, I found myself on White Oak Mountain in southern Virginia in search of ancestral graves. The vista commanded a rolling countryside, watered by the springs of the Shenandoah, a land my family had known for nearly three centuries. Across the mountain clearing I spotted a row of sunken graves and unsettled headstones. Most of the inscriptions had been effaced by time, but I was struck by one crumbling stone that read, "GONE BUT NOT FORGOTTEN." At first I chuckled a bit at this, considering the rutted roads I had traveled, the strangers I had queried, and the brambles I had wrestled just to find this forsaken place. And yet I knew that I *had* remembered; I had kept faith with that simple, hopeful declaration, "Gone but not forgotten." There has always been something special to me about finding ancestral graves, something that goes beyond the clerical work that is a necessary part of being a genealogist, for it pays respect to fathers and mothers of long past. It also gives a tangibility to the names and dates of the family chronicle.

Climbing Your Family Tree

Handcarved slate, 1841,
Danville, Virginia

Brick vaults, Early American

Limestone, 1793,
Argyle, New York

Figure 5-1 *Styles and materials of grave markers*

Cast iron infant grave coverings,
1850, Danville, Virginia

Marble with elaborate mourning pictorial,
1848, Hillsborough, North Carolina

SACRED
TO THE MEMORY
OF
MARY SCHAW,
wife of
LUCIAN HOLMES,
who died
March 9, 1849,
Aged 24 years.

She needs no formal
record of her virtues on
this cold marble. They
are deeply graven on the
tablets of many warm
and loving hearts, in
which her memory is
tenderly enshrined and
sacredly cherished.

Elegy "on this cold marble,"
1849, Hillsborough, North Carolina

Climbing Your Family Tree

The sepulchral subject of cemeteries is really a fascinating aspect of the genealogist's work. Besides the enjoyment of the hunt for cemeteries that may lead you to moss-draped churchyards and forgotten little family plots, critical answers may also be carved in stone there, for tombstones at times are the only record remaining about some of your ancestors.

The Stones Speak

The typical cemetery of today's metropolitan America generally reflects the nature of the city—large and impersonal. Bearing such pleasant euphemisms as "Memorial Gardens" and "Hills of Rest," these cemeteries sometimes more closely resemble a golf course than a graveyard. In contrast, older burial places have characteristics of arrangement and style of headstones that provide helpful chronological clues for the genealogist; consequently, we shall take a brief look at this grave subject.

During our nation's early years until the twentieth century, the two primary places for burial were the churchyard and the family plot. Of course, these are still in use today; however, increasingly during the nineteenth century, towns and cities provided cemetery space for their residents. During the twentieth century, particularly during the postwar period, the large, commercial, suburban cemetery became common. For purposes of genealogical research, we will focus on the earlier burial settings.

Old gravestones reflect their times as well as the financial means of the families involved. From the colonial period until about the 1850s, slate and soapstone were the most common tombstone materials. The softness of these stones made it easy for local artisans to carve the epitaphs. Though their skills varied considerably, some of these unknown craftsmen have left behind exquisite decorative carvings, some of which have weathered well over two centuries. From 1830 to 1850 a gradual change is evident as improved stonecutting technology permitted the use of harder materials, particularly marble, and more standardized die-cut lettering.

During the late nineteenth century, for those with means, Victorian styles prevailed as much in the cemetery as they did in the parlor. Elaborate marble carvings, embellished epitaphs, and creative arrangements of family plots can often be found in the century-old corner of a city cemetery. I once came upon such a Victorian style plot for a family that had really gone out in style. In the middle of the plot was a marble tree stump symbolizing life cut off by death; the roots of the tree led to various pedestals surrounding the stump, marking the family graves. On one pedestal carved in marble was a dashing derby hat, on another an open book, and on still another a squirrel eating a nut. Unfortunately, the last time I visited that cemetery nearly every gravestone there had been thrown over and broken by vandals. Such senseless destruction perpetrated by petty criminals who have no respect for the living or the dead poses an ever-increasing threat to the historical treasures in our nation's old cemeteries.

If you come across a headstone during your family history research that is a towering obelisk of marble filled with genealogical detail, count your blessings. Oftentimes you will find old family graves marked by simple stones with simple inscriptions or even less—a fieldstone, a rotting wooden cross or stake or even *nothing*. I once tracked down the name and location of the church where my great-great grandfather was buried in 1890. When I arrived, the only parishioners I found were grazing cattle. Not a trace of the church remained, and my ancestor's grave had long since become a forgotten part of a rolling, green pasture.

Besides the genealogical information available on tombstones, the earlier epitaphs are at times poignant and poetic. Unlike most epitaphs today that provide only the barest of vital statistics, rich eulogies such as the epitaph of Pvt. Harry

Miller in Pendleton, South Carolina, can be found among the last words in century-old cemeteries:

> The youthful Soldier
> impatient of the dull
> routine within the Halls of
> Chapel Hill in the month of
> August, 1862 and at the
> age of 17 bade adieu to
> the duties of College life
> and with patriotic ardor and
> alacrity sought the more
> exciting scenes of the tented
> field, amid the Camps
> of the Confederate Army.
> Then quartered around
> the City of Richmond.
> The Battle of Malvern Hill
> soon transformed the student
> of camp-drill, into the trained
> Soldier: and thenceforward with
> veteran steadiness, he followed
> the fortunes of the Army of
> Northern Virginia, until the
> 9th of Oct. 1864,
> when during a triumphant
> assault upon the third line
> of the enemy's breast-works,
> at Middletown, Va., by
> Gen. Kershaw's old Brigade, he
> fell a noble sacrifice to the
> cause he had so generously
> and earnestly espoused.
>
> This column of marble
> with its speaking emblems

is the offering of a Father's
affection and devotion
and is erected as a memento
of the noble self-sacrificing
example of a Patriotic Son.

The epitaphs that speak of courage, sorrow, or hope all provide a glimpse into the lives of the departed and those left behind. I am often impressed with the living faith so evident among the death and decay of a graveyard not only in the epitaphs but at times even with the positioning of the headstones. Many old tombstones face east, not simply to greet the rising sun, but for believers, to face the Son of God on the Resurrection morning. These saints at rest are confident of the promise in Malachi 4:2, "But unto you that fear my name shall the Sun of righteousness arise with healing in his wings."

The Search

The search for ancestral graves begins with older relatives. Be sure to make detailed questions about burial locations a part of your interviews. It is best if a knowledgeable relative can actually accompany you to the cemetery, for being there in person can often awaken old memories and generate fresh stories. Also since some graves, particularly those of infants, may be marked with only an initialed stone, the relative may be helpful in deciphering a cryptic crypt.

If your only leads to an ancestor's grave are a name and a town, ask around for the location of old cemeteries. Some cemeteries maintain records of burial locations, but if these are not available, you may be able to narrow your search by estimating the death date of your ancestor and considering the styles of grave markers as noted earlier. While in town, it is also worth finding out whether there is a town historian. Small-town historians such as Mary Wilson of Lake Mills,

Wisconsin, are a remarkable, hardy breed. Unpaid and underappreciated, they find music in the rhythms of community life. These historical caretakers of America's counties and crossroads villages can often be helpful in providing encouragement, anecdotes, and, best of all, directions.

If the family cemetery is in a rural area and you have only vague directions, look for clumps of trees in the middle of plowed fields, or for cedar trees, which were often planted in family plots. Of course, do not be afraid to explain yourself and ask questions among the residents of the area. Once, after a frustrating search across field and stream, I asked a farmer if he knew about any graves on the land. Not only did he direct me to the family plot of my great-great-great-grandfather, but also he showed me where my ancestor's log cabin had stood. I even found the foundation stones that had been laid in the 1840s. I had also found a "new" relative, for as it turned out, my helpful farmer and I shared the same ancestor—we were distant cousins.

When you find ancestral graves, make careful notes about their locations and enter them on the Family Data Sheet. Be sure to include road names or numbers, and if you are literally off the beaten path, sketch out a map of your trek.

Wearing protective clothing is also an important consideration in grave hunting since briars, ticks, and chiggers may plague your trail to abandoned sites. Gloves and hedge trimmers are helpful for clearing grave sites for photographing. If old graves lie in a wooded area, a spade may also be useful to clear the compost formed by the leaves of a hundred autumns that often obscure the lower lines of an epitaph. The important thing is to be prepared and to be *aware*. Not long ago I found what was likely the grave of my great-great-great-grandmother, marked by only a rough fieldstone. I reached down to prop up the toppled marker. As I pulled it up, between my fingers glimmered a gossamer thread clutched at the other end by a large black widow spider that seemed not to share my interest in genealogical research. Suddenly I became more interested in the present than the past and let both the gravestone and the spider rest in peace.

Recording

Both written and photographic records should be made of ancestral gravesites. Carefully record the epitaphs and recheck the copy against the inscription to insure accuracy. Keep in mind, however, that stonecutters were not infallible; whenever possible compare the epitaph information with other sources. Photograph both the general disposition of the cemetery and individual headstones, and include these pictures in the family chronicle. Be sure to take close-up photographs of the epitaph and give consideration to the lighting. If it is an overcast day or you are shooting in a heavily wooded area, use a fill-flash. If bright sunlight is bearing down, use a polarizing filter to reduce the glare on the stone.

While all this sounds simple enough, and at times it is, there are often the inevitable ravages of time that can complicate your efforts. A soft stone washed by a century or more of rain and snow, and covered by moss or lichens, is often a real challenge to decipher. There are, however, several things you can do to capture these fading last words. First, if the stone is lichen-covered, use a coarse cloth soaked in vinegar to rub the fungus off the inscription. Under *no circumstances* should a wire brush be used to scrub the stone. This unwise and unprofessional method of cleaning has done much damage to fading epitaphs. Marble, a form of limestone, calcifies and crumbles when acid contacts it. The natural acids present in lichens and the acids present in precipitation often leave exposed marble surfaces "rough," permitting the wires of a scrub brush to dig deeper into the soft surface. A maxim for grave-hunters should be always to leave a cemetery in at least as good a condition as they found it. And if the cemetery has been neglected, show it some care.

A second method for recording fading inscriptions is to rub cornstarch over the surface. As the powder settles into the letters, they become more legible. Rubbings made with crayon or pencil on paper laid on the tombstone are useful in recording epitaphs. Rubbings may also capture artwork such as weeping willows, skulls, crosses, or symbols of fraternal societies. Use white or buff paper of regular weight, but be sure that a single sheet is large enough to avoid the problem of piecing several together. Tissue paper may also be used for rubbings, but it should be stored on a roll to reduce wrinkling. Nonfusable medium-weight fabric interfacing, such as Pellon, is a versatile rubbing surface that may be folded. If crayon is used for rubbing over the fabric, you may apply a warm iron afterward to fix the image on the cloth. Pellon has many advantages as a rubbing surface, including the ability to hand-launder it after fixing the image with an iron, and it can be purchased in long pieces which can accommodate a number of rubbings.

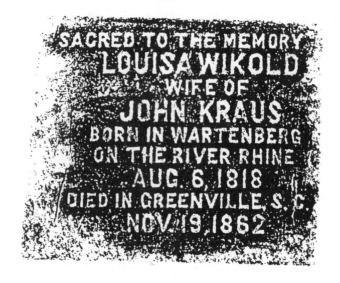

Figure 5-2 *Tombstone rubbing on Pellon*

2

1

Oakes Cemetery
1/2 mile walk from County Rd.806
near Tomahawk Creek, Pittsylvania County, Va.

1. W. O. Born
    Jan 7th 1780
    D Nov 24
    1846

2. ELISEBETH
   GIBSON was
   BORN MAY 22th (sic)
   1835 DEC oct th8
   1861

3. fieldstone marker

4. fieldstone marker

5. fieldstone marker

6. REBECCA J. OAKES
   BORN
   Sep. 6, 1855
   Died
   Apr. 3, 1909
   At Rest

7. MARGRATE C
   wife of
   James A. Oakes
   Born
   Mar. 15, 1823
   Died
   Dec. 4, 1909

8. MARY C. OAKES
   Born
   July 22, 1848
   Died
   June 4, 1914

9. JAMES H. OAKES
   OCT 23, 1846
   JAN 25, 1928
   May he rest in
   peace

10. Almira O Reynolds
    July. 15, 1853
    Jan. 27, 1944
    Not Dead But
    Sleepeth

Figure 5-3 Grave site diagram

Climbing Your Family Tree

Another means of recording and examining the genealogical information at a family group cemetery is by diagramming the arrangement of the graves. As Figure 5-3 illustrates, sketch the layout and show the shape of the gravestones, both headstones and footstones. Designate a letter for each grave and key it into a copy of the epitaph included with the diagram. Such a sketch will permit you to study afterward how the cemetery arrangement evolved and the relationship of the graves to each other. Such close examination can often raise interesting questions and open up new trails to follow. For example, if other families are buried in a small cemetery, look at the grave arrangements to see if there are marriage ties between the family groups. You may actually discover long-forgotten relatives that will lead you further along on your exciting quest into the past.

6
Public Sources

As you climb your family tree, you will soon come to more distant branches that neither memory nor existing family records will permit you to reach. It is time then to look to county and state records which are critical to genealogical research. This chapter will introduce the subjects of vital records (birth, marriage, and death records) and census records. Researching your family's past through public records requires patience, carefulness, and doggedness, but such research is indispensable and the results invaluable.

Before examining specific areas of public records, you should keep in mind a few cautions and considerations. First, the fundamental characteristic of public records is that they originate and are organized in a geographic context. In other words, if your ancestor married and raised a family in, for example, East Canton, Ohio, you must obtain the marriage information and other vital information from the appropriate Ohio county, in this case Stark County. The information must be obtained either in person or through some form of mechanical transfer such as acquiring photocopies of records by mail from the county courthouse or by examining available microfilm copies through interlibrary loan.

Second, when visiting a county records office or using the genealogical facilities of a public library, do not be afraid to ask questions about what records are available and how they are indexed. A few questions at the beginning may save you valuable time at the end. When asking for help from clerks or library assistants, be considerate of their time. They probably won't find your enthusiasm for your subject particularly contagious, and they often have many other responsibilities. Some even may have had bad experiences with pushy genealogists, derisively referred to as *genies*. Simple politeness will usually smooth the way for some much needed direction among the bewildering maze of public records.

Reading Writing

Another practical consideration that will sooner or later plague your research through public records is the problem of deciphering poor, archaic, or fading penmanship. Despite the beauty and grace of early American documents, epitomized in the style of the Declaration of Independence, not all clerks were so gifted. Experience is the best teacher in reading old writing, but we will consider some prevalent pitfalls you will encounter as you work your way through the old tomes. The two most common problems involving lower-case letters are the double *s* and the similarity between *m*, *n*, *u*, and *w*. In documents prior to the Civil War, both written and printed, the first *s* in the double *s* looks like an *f*.

In documents prior to the eighteenth century, every *s* in a word including the first lower-case *s* letter was printed as an *f* with the exception of the last *s* of a word ending in *s*, as follows:

33 🟥euertheleſſe, my loüing kinde⸗
neſſe will J not vtterly take from him:
no₂ † ſuffer my faithfulneſſe † to faile.

The chief quill culprits among upper case letters are the letters *I*, *J*, and *T*. These letters are often confusing in their similarity. In fact, *I* and *J* are identical in some handwriting. This probably reflects the fact that the letter *J* is a relative newcomer to our alphabet. Words that contain *J*'s today used *I*'s in earlier forms. For example, in the following verse from a 1582 edition of the Geneva Bible, note that the first letter of Israel and the first letter of Jephthah are identical.

40 The daughters of Jſrael went yꝰre by
ẏꝰre to lament the daughter of Jphtah
the Gileadite, foure dayes in a yeere.

The elegant, flowing style of eighteenth- and nineteenth-century handwriting was largely the result of the Spencerian style handwriting taught in primary schools of that day. In print the script appeared as follows:

$$\mathcal{A} \; \mathcal{B} \; \mathcal{C} \; \mathcal{D} \; \mathcal{E} \; \mathcal{F} \; \mathcal{G} \; \mathcal{H} \; \mathcal{I} \; \mathcal{J}$$
$$\mathcal{K} \; \mathcal{L} \; \mathcal{M} \; \mathcal{N} \; \mathcal{O} \; \mathcal{P} \; \mathcal{Q} \; \mathcal{R}$$
$$\mathcal{S} \; \mathcal{T} \; \mathcal{U} \; \mathcal{V} \; \mathcal{W} \; \mathcal{X} \; \mathcal{Y} \; \mathcal{Z}$$

Climbing Your Family Tree

If you have difficulty with a word, compare the problem letters with similar examples elsewhere in the document. The context may also provide a clue. If the problem word cannot be satisfactorily cleared up and you are copying the document, leave a blank and in parentheses write out your best guess or guesses. The "word" may look like nonsense, but the answer may turn up after you step back from your work and take a fresh look later.

Date Debate

One other problem you may face in the old records involves dates. Over the years man's methods of framing time have shifted between the moon and the sun and have been shaped by his science and politics. The Egyptians were the earliest of the ancients to cease measuring years by the moon. Because of the sun's peculiar relationship to the rising Nile, they found it, not the waxing and waning moon, to be a superior standard for marking a year.

Long before the birth of Moses, the Egyptians calculated a 365-day year much as we do today. A solar year was so superior to lunar calculations that Julius Caesar adopted the Egyptian calendar, fine tuned it to 365 1/4 days, and put his name on it.

For over sixteen centuries the Julian calendar reigned throughout Europe. However, its 365-day year with a quadrennial "leap" of 366 days was gradually gaining time, being off by eleven minutes and fourteen seconds from the actual solar round of 365 days, 5 hours, 48 minutes, and 46 seconds. Like grains gathering in a glass, over the centuries the extra minutes took their toll in time. By the sixteenth century Pope Gregory XIII undertook to correct the calendar by decree. Gregory advanced the calendar by ten days (October 4, 1582, was followed by October 15) and then to maintain the correction declared that only the double zero years evenly divided by 400 (e.g., 1600 and 2000) would be leap years. In addition the pope changed New Year's Day from March 25 to January 1. (March 25—nine months before Christmas—is Annunciation Day commemorating Gabriel's announcement to the Virgin Mary that she would give birth to the Messiah.) As we shall see, this shift in the date of New Year's Day has a significant effect on the genealogist's reckoning.

There was only one problem with the Gregorian calendar—it bore the name of a Catholic. It was a day of Reformation and religious war, and Gregory was no spectator. When word reached Rome of the St. Bartholomew Day's Massacre, in which thousands of Protestants were murdered in one ghastly night, Pope Gregory filled the messenger's pockets with gold florins and declared a day of public thanksgiving. Naturally Protestants and Catholics were as divided over matters of time as they were over matters of eternity. As a result, Protestant England and America did not change from the Old Style Julian calendar to the New Style Gregorian calendar until 1752. By then the gap was eleven days so that September 2 was followed by September 14. Frettings over the "loss" of wages and time were assuaged by the wit of Ben Franklin, who comforted readers of *Poor Richard's Almanack* with these words:

Be not astonished, nor look with scorn, dear reader, at such a deduction of days, nor regret as for the loss of so much time, but take this for your consolation, that your expenses will appear lighter and your mind be more at ease. And what an indulgence is here, for those who love their pillow to lie down in peace on the second of this month and not perhaps awake till the morning of the fourteenth.

The difference between Old Style (O.S.) and New Style (N.S.) dating is significant for the genealogist. What may appear to be discrepancies in dating may be explained by the calendar change. This is particularly true regarding the two New Year's Days (March 25, Julian; January 1, Gregorian) of the two systems. For example, if you had christening dates of siblings listed chronologically in a church register as April 5, 1734, and March 20, 1734, you might wrongly conclude there was a scribal error. Under the Julian calendar, of course, these dates are over eleven months apart. To reconcile the "year problem" brought on by the New Year's Day shift, double years are recorded for years prior to 1752 for dates that fall on or between January 1 and March 24. This means that the date in the above example should be recorded in your chronicle as March 20, 1734/35.

County Lines

An additional consideration in tracking down public records is the changing face of the map. For the most part, vital records of birth, marriage, and death were gathered in local jurisdictions. This means that locating the counties where your ancestors lived is an important step in locating all available records. But counties were once bits of territories, and territories frontier, and frontier was once wilderness. As Figure 6-1 illustrates, counties, particularly in the East, sometimes have their own family tree. Counties were carved out of larger counties which were really just rough divisions of the frontier. The smaller county jurisdiction made a little more manageable what the rough and tumble wilderness needed most—law and order.

For genealogists, knowing the where and when of county lines can save time by narrowing the search to the appropriate courthouse archive. The whole issue of local jurisdiction underscores the fact that records are not always found where you expect them. If your initial county research turns up empty, neighboring counties may have the information you need.

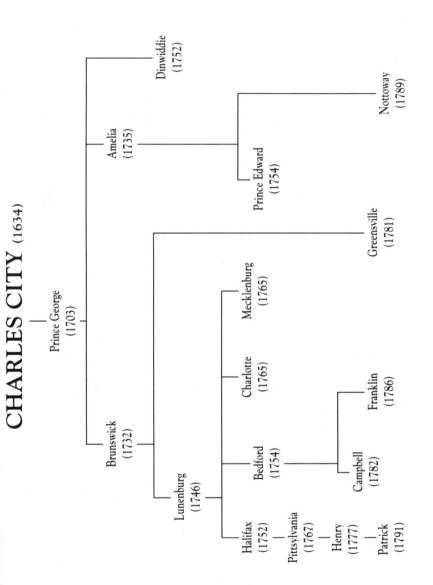

Figure 6-1 *County "family tree" for Charles City, Virginia*

Cradle to Grave

We live in an age of numbers. You may, for example, attempt to make a single purchase with a check. After getting your driver's license number, credit card number, and your nine-digit zip code ready for inspection, if you are not careful, you may be told to get in line and take a number! Somehow our ancestors managed to survive quite well without so many numbers, carbon forms, or plastic cards. For the genealogist, however, the lack of records or record-keeping systems makes the search for names and dates more difficult—or perhaps more challenging. Nowhere is this more true than in the records of life's most basic issues—the beginning and ending, birth and death.

The earliest vital records in America were the christening registers in early Virginia and Massachusetts parishes. Colonial governments eventually took responsibility for collecting birth and death information, but the records are spotty because the enforcement was sporadic. As late as 1833 only five cities in the country had a system of vital registration: New Orleans, Baltimore, Philadelphia, New York, and Boston. Though Massachusetts's state-wide system in 1844 was a notable exception, in most cases the law was on the books, but few records were. It was 1875, for example, before death certificates were required in Baltimore.

Even today, there is no national system of vital registration. The recording of births, deaths, and marriages is largely a state matter. Since 1900, state records are fairly thorough, although vital registration in rural outlays remained sketchy until after World War II. Perhaps the best source for tracking down birth and death dates is to consult a Department of Health and Human Services booklet entitled *Where to Write for Vital Records,* available for a nominal sum from the Superintendent of Documents, U.S. Government Printing Office, Washington, DC 20402.

The Bonds of Matrimony

Marriage records are among the most valuable tools of the genealogist's craft. In many cases births were not recorded officially, but marriage was a ceremony, partly religious and partly civil. Therefore, a state record of the event likely exists. Marriage records, particularly those after 1830, often provide a resource of answers including age, occupation, and most importantly, the names of parents.

Federalism in America, the division of political power between two or more levels, affects everything from how taxes are collected to how marriages are recorded. Since there have never been any uniform national codes regarding marriage records, they have varied over time and from state to state and, in some cases, from county to county. Fittingly, the two men who had the most to do with tying the nuptial knot, representing God and Caesar, were the minister and the village clerk.

This community quality of the wedding is reflected in America's earliest marriage records, known as banns. Banns, an import from the old country, were public announcements of a couple's betrothal either announced from the pulpit or posted by a town clerk. The purpose was to allow members of the community time to raise objections to the proposal before the marriage was consummated. This colonial custom still survives in some marriage vows today, when the preacher announces "If any know just cause why these two persons should not be joined together in holy matrimony, let him speak now or forever hold his peace." If nervous nuptialists cringe during this "invitation," perhaps they might take a little comfort from the realization that banns used to last for a month rather than a second!

Marriage bonds are the most common marriage records of antebellum America, particularly in New England and the South. The bridegroom posted the bond in the county where the wedding was to be held, and the bride's father or brother usually cosigned it. The bond bound with penalty the bridegroom in case of an annulment. The date of the marriage bond was often a few days before the ceremony, but the actual wedding date was not always noted.

In some states during certain periods, posting bond was all that was required and is thus the only written record that exists. Since the bond had to be signed by the groom and often also by the bride's father, the signatures of two direct ancestors usually adorn these old documents. Photocopies of these autographs make a fine addition to the family chronicle. The absence of a signature also tells you something about your distant forebears. If next to the clerk's annotation "His Mark" there is a large *X,* you will know that your ancestor was illiterate—a common condition in early America.

Marriage licenses gradually replaced bonds, though in some jurisdictions both were required. Among the earliest states to issue marriage licenses were Indiana and Wisconsin, but by the post–Civil War period, most other states had followed suit.

60   **Figure 6-2** *Marriage bond, 1811*

The license application often contains a wealth of information such as full names, parents' names, birthplaces, occupations, and previous marriages. This last item can sometimes produce surprises as I learned when I found my great-great-grandmother's 1865 marriage license. The license revealed that she was a young war widow—one of the hundred thousand that the War of Brothers produced.

Generally, the minister had the responsibility of reporting the ceremony to civil authorities, although this does not

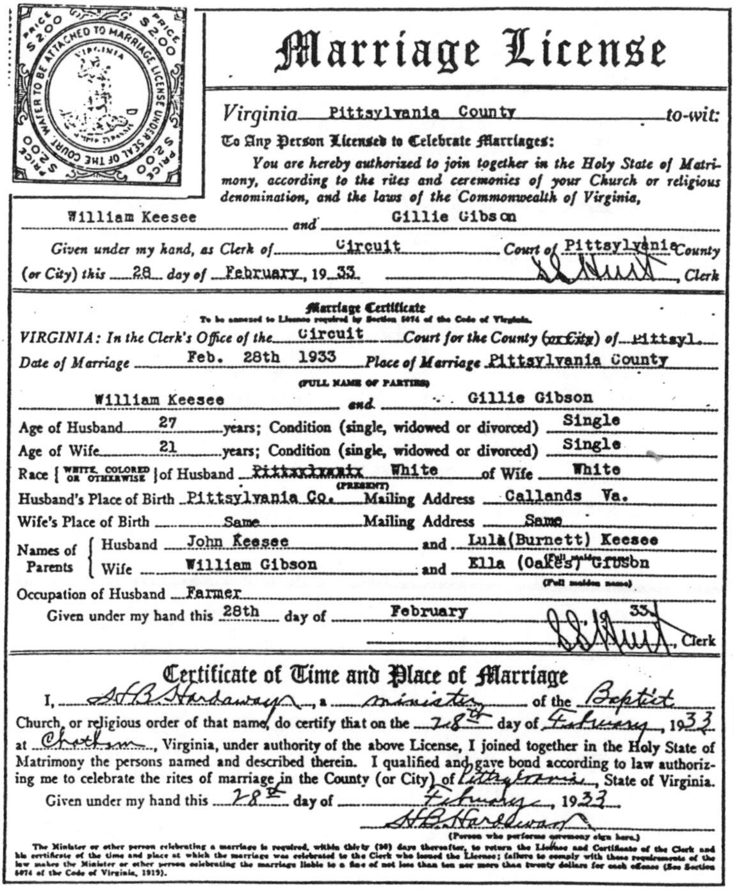

Marriage License

Virginia Pittsylvania County *to-wit:*

To Any Person Licensed to Celebrate Marriages:

You are hereby authorized to join together in the Holy State of Matrimony, according to the rites and ceremonies of your Church or religious denomination, and the laws of the Commonwealth of Virginia,

William Keesee *and* Gillie Gibson

Given under my hand, as Clerk of Circuit *Court of* Pittsylvania *County (or City) this* 28 *day of* February, 19 33.

, Clerk

Marriage Certificate

To be annexed to License required by Section 5074 of the Code of Virginia.

VIRGINIA: In the Clerk's Office of the Circuit *Court for the County (or City) of* Pittsyl.

Date of Marriage Feb. 28th 1933 *Place of Marriage* Pittsylvania County

(FULL NAME OF PARTIES)

William Keesee *and* Gillie Gibson

Age of Husband 27 years; Condition (single, widowed or divorced) Single

Age of Wife 21 years; Condition (single, widowed or divorced) Single

Race { WHITE, COLORED OR OTHERWISE } of Husband White of Wife White

Husband's Place of Birth Pittsylvania Co. (PRESENT) Mailing Address Callands Va.

Wife's Place of Birth Same Mailing Address Same

Names of Parents { Husband John Keesee and Lula (Burnett) Keesee

Wife William Gibson and Ella (Oakes) Gibson (Full maiden name)

Occupation of Husband Farmer

Given under my hand this 28th day of February 19 33

, Clerk

Certificate of Time and Place of Marriage

I, S. H. B. Hardaway, a minister of the Baptist Church, or religious order of that name, do certify that on the 28th day of February, 1933 at Chatham, Virginia, under authority of the above License, I joined together in the Holy State of Matrimony the persons named and described therein. I qualified and gave bond according to law authorizing me to celebrate the rites of marriage in the County (or City) of Pittsylvania, State of Virginia.

Given under my hand this 28th day of February, 1933.

S. H. B. Hardaway

(Person who performs ceremony sign here.)

The Minister or other person celebrating a marriage is required, within thirty (30) days thereafter, to return the License and Certificate of the Clerk and his certificate of the time and place at which the marriage was celebrated to the Clerk who issued the License; failure to comply with these requirements of the law makes the Minister or other person celebrating the marriage liable to a fine of not less than ten nor more than twenty dollars for each offense (See Section 5074 of the Code of Virginia, 1919).

Figure 6-3 *Marriage license, 1933*

REGISTER C

Within the County of Pittsylvania, for the Y

Line Number	Date	Town or County	Husband	Wife	Husband Age Yrs.	Wife Age Yrs.	Single or Widowed Husband	Wife	Color	Husband Place
1	1879 June 14	Pitts. Co	Stephen Smith	Flora Anderson	21	25	Single	Single	Cold	Pittsylvania Co
2	" " 17	"	F.G. Slate	Susan A. Dodson	27	17	"	"	Wht	"
3	July 9	"	Sidney B Dixon	Ally le Hivier	23	18	"	"	W	
4	June 8	"	John P Davenport	Hattie R Lovelace	37	25	"	"	W	Halifax "
5	" " 22	"	Geo P Soler	Narcissa James	18	14	"	"	Col	Pittsylvania
6	" 25	"	J.S. Carter	Julia W. Garris	24	21	"	"	White	Halifax
7	" 26	"	Temple Darr	R.J. Wilson	19	17	"	"	"	Pitts
8	" 28	"	Logan Adams	Mary Ferguson	32	22	Widowed	Widowed	Cold	"
9	July 22	"	George P Motley	Mattie A Burch	40	16	"	Single	White	"
10	" 3	"	John C Anderson	Mollie A Smith	26	20	Single	"	"	"
11		"	David Brooke	Harriett J Williams						
12	" 6	"	Calohil Allen	Emily Smith	21	19	"	"	Cold	"
13	" 20	"	Reid Miller	Hester Gilbert	24	19	"	"	"	"
14	" 20	"	Andrew Wilson	Mary Tarnill	25	20	"	"	"	"
15	" 17	"	John Wilson	Lilly Wilson	24	21	"	"	"	"

mean that he always fulfilled his responsibility. This was particularly true if the minister was a circuit rider crossing several county lines in his charge. In some cases a license was applied for in one county, the ceremony took place in another, and the minister filed the return in his home county.

Figure 6-3 illustrates a typical marriage license of the late nineteenth century through the early twentieth century. The minister's handwritten return at the close of the document reports that the vows were duly solemnized.

The marriage register was the civil record of marriage. (See Figure 6-4.) These large tomes housed in county or town courthouses are indexed by both bride's and groom's surnames and are well worth examining. Although the information is sometimes sketchier than that found in the marriage license, the register often contains records of lateral relations. Since registers are indexed chronologically by name in an alphabetical listing, the marriage records of

Figure 6-4 *Marriage register, 1879*

ARRIAGES

ng on the thirty-first day of December, 1879 .

s OF THEIR RESIDENCE:		NAMES OF THEIR PARENTS.		OCCUPATION OF HUSBAND.	NAME OF PERSON PERFORM- ING MARRIAGE CEREMONY.	WHEN ISSUED.
	WIFE.	HUSBAND.	WIFE.			
	Petta Lee	Wm Smith & Victoria Lewis	James Pannell & ——	Farmer	Lev. Wr.	1879 June 10th
	"	Not Known	Aley & Martha Dodson	Merchant	Rev. W. Wood	" 16th
	"	E W & D Dixon	W J & Sallie F. Hines	Farmer	J. S. Southall	June 16
	"	Jno D. & Susan Davenport	Mathew & —— Lovelace	Farmer	Geo. Dunn	" 18th
	"	Abr. Craft & Sallie Foley	George & Bettie Lasster	"	Wm S. McDowell	" 21
	"	J S & S G. Carter	B R & J. A. Farris	"	E. B. Dillard	" 23
	"	Stephen & Eliz H Davis	Jack & Rebecca A Wilson	"	John R. Roark	" 24
	"	Benj Adams & Matilda	Daniel Keatts & ——	Carpenter	Peter Wilson	" 28
	"	William & Martha M. Motley	John W. & Nannie J Burch	Tobacconist	He. Petty	" 28th
	"	Watoley & Nancy Anderson	William & Rebecca Smith	Physician	Wm. He. Matthews	July 13
	"	Not Known	Jane Williams & Hyram Stumps		E. B. Chaney	" 2
	"	Richard & Sobrey Allen	—— & Rachel Smith	Farmer	B. A. Davis	" 4
	"	Not Known	Reuben & Miely Gilbert		S. W. Sims	" 14
	"	—— & Elizth. Ross	Sandy & Isabella Pannell	Ferryman	Benjamin Ken	" 12
	"	Glasgow & —— Wilson	Champ & Mary Wilson	Farmer	Lindon Coleman	" 15

brothers and sisters to your direct ancestor may turn up in your search.

Census

In the summer of 1787, temperatures in Philadelphia were hot and tempers were hotter, as deadlocked debate threatened the survival of the Constitutional Convention. Delegates from small and large states argued over how representation would be determined. At last a compromise was reached that made representation in the Senate equal for each state, regardless of its size. Representation in the House, however, would be based on population. This little political maneuver, known as the Great Compromise, had big results. The compromise mandated not only the structure of our national legislature but also the numbering of people every ten years, necessary to determine representation based on population. The resulting censuses taken since 1790 are a gold mine for genealogists.

At first, the census could be described as strict constructionist. The 1790 Census does little more than name the heads of households and number the people free and bond. As you can see, however, from the following census descriptions taken from the Census Bureau's *Factfinder of the Nation*, the decennial count became increasingly sophisticated.

1790 Census—Name of family head; free white males of 16 years and up, free white males under 16, free white females; slaves; other persons.

1800 Census—Name of family head; if white, age and sex; race; slaves.

1810 Census—Name of family head; if white, age and sex; race; slaves.

1820 Census—Name of family head; age; sex; race; foreigners not naturalized; slaves; industry (whether agriculture, commerce, or manufacturing).

1830 Census—Name of family head; age; sex; race; slaves; deaf and dumb; blind; foreigners not naturalized.

1840 Census—Name of family head; age; sex; race; slaves; number of deaf and dumb; number of blind; number of insane and idiotic and whether in public or private charge; number of persons in each family employed in each of six classes of industry and one of occupation; literacy; pensioners for Revolutionary or military service.

1850 Census—Name; age; sex; race; whether deaf and dumb, blind, insane, or idiotic; value of real estate; occupation; birthplace; whether married within the year; school attendance; literacy; whether a pauper or convict. Supplemental schedules for slaves; public paupers and criminals; persons who died during the year.

1860 Census—Name; age; sex; race; value of real estate; value of personal estate; occupation; birthplace; whether married within the year; school attendance; literacy; whether deaf and dumb, blind, insane, idiotic, pauper, or convict; number of slave houses. Supplemental schedules for slaves; public paupers and criminals; persons who died during the year.

1870 Census—Name; age; race; occupation; value of real estate; value of personal estate; birthplace; whether parents were foreign born; months of birth if born within the year; month of marriage if married within the year; school attendance; literacy; whether deaf and dumb, blind, insane, or idiotic; male citizens 21 and over, and number of such persons denied the right to vote for reasons other than rebellion. Supplemental schedules for persons who died during the year; paupers; prisoners.

1880 Census—Address; name; relationship to family head; sex; race; age; marital status; month of birth if born within the census year; occupation; months unemployed during the year; sickness or temporary disability; whether blind, deaf and dumb, idiotic, insane, maimed, crippled, bedridden, or otherwise disabled; school attendance; literacy; birthplace of person and parents. Supplemental schedules for the Indian population; for persons who died during the year; insane; idiots; deaf-mutes; blind; homeless children; prisoners; paupers and indigent persons.

1890 Census—Largely destroyed by fire, only scattered records extant.

1900 Census—Address; name; relationship to family head; sex; race; age; marital status; number of years married; for women, number of children born and number now living;

birthplace of persons and parents; if foreign born, year of immigration and whether naturalized; occupation; months not employed; school attendance; literacy; ability to speak English; whether on a farm; home owned or rented and if owned, whether mortgaged. Supplemental schedules for the blind and for the deaf.

1910 Census—Address; names; relationship to family head; sex; race; age; marital status; number of years of present marriage; for women, number of children born and number now living; birthplace and mother tongue of person and parents; if foreign born, year of immigration, whether naturalized, and whether able to speak English, or, if not, language spoken; occupation, industry, and class of worker; if an employee, whether out of work during year; literacy; school attendance; home owned or rented; if owned, whether mortgaged; whether farm or house; whether a survivor of Union or Confederate Army or Navy; whether blind or deaf and dumb.

1920 Census—Address; name; relationship to family head, sex; race; age; marital status; if foreign born, year of immigration to the U.S., whether naturalized, and year of naturalization; school attendance; literacy; birthplace of person and parents; mother tongue of foreign born; ability to speak English; occupation, industry, and class of worker; home owned or rented; if owned, whether mortgaged; for nonfarm mortgaged, market value, original amount of mortgage, balance due, interest rate.

1930 Census—Address; name; relationship to family head; home owned or rented; value or monthly rental; radio set; whether on a farm; sex; race; age; marital status; age at first marriage; school attendance; literacy; birthplace of persons and parents; if foreign born, language spoken in home before coming to U.S., year of immigration, whether naturalized, and ability to speak English; occupation, industry, and class of worker; whether at work previous day (or last regular working day); veteran status; for Indians, whether of full or mixed blood, and tribal affiliation.

1940 Census—Address; home owned or rented; value or monthly rental; whether on a farm; name; relationship to household head; sex; race; age; marital status; school attendance; education attainment; birthplace; citizenship of foreign born; location of residence 5 years ago and whether on a farm; employment status, if at work; whether in private or nonemergency government work, hours worked in week; if seeking work or on public emergency work, duration of unemployment; occupation, industry, and class of worker; weeks worked last year; income last year.

1950 Census—Address; whether house is on farm; name; relationship to household head; race; sex; age; marital status; birthplace; if foreign born, whether naturalized; employment status; hours worked in week; occupation, industry, and class of worker.

For the genealogist, the 1850 Census represents a particularly significant step since household members, not just heads of household, are listed by name and age. This particular record of my great-great-great-grandmother (Figure 6-5, line 8) offers information between the lines. Drusy Griffith married Ellis Jones in 1839. After ten years of marriage, Drusy Jones is listed in the 1850 census records as a twenty-nine-year-old head of household with an eight-month-old boy named Ellis among her brood of four. This means that Ellis Sr. was alive until the summer of 1849. Did Drusy give her son the name Ellis because her husband died while she was expecting? Clues, questions, and curiosity are all part of the family historian's craft.

Because of the comprehensive indexes that are available today, the federal censuses are quite accessible. It is helpful to know the county an ancestor was from, particularly if his

68   Figure 6-5   *1850 census entry for Drusy Jones*

was a common name. However, even if you know only the state he hailed from, with a little digging you can usually find him. The index will indicate the particular microfilm reel that may either be obtained (if your library has a good genealogical division) or ordered through interlibrary loan. Appendix B lists the regional Federal Records Centers that house census records. These branches of the National Archives may be helpful when tracking down material through your local library.

As you turn to the census for information, keep in mind two things. First, no census is complete, whether it was conducted in 1790 or 1990. Sometimes people were missed in the count, or records were lost or destroyed. Second, only census records older than seventy-four years are in public domain. A narrow search through more recent records is possible if you are a direct blood relation and fill out the necessary government paperwork. For information and forms, write to the Bureau of the Census, Pittsburg, Kansas 66762.

Crossing the Ocean

America being a land of immigrants, the roots of most of its family trees stretch to foreign shores. Since the early seventeenth century when Englishmen stood with the wilderness before them and the ocean behind them, men and women have continued to come—fifty million of them since 1607, from every continent and walk of life.

A good place to begin your attempt to reach the Old World are ships' passenger lists. Most official lists from 1820 to 1945 are available on microfilm at the National Archives. Two basic guides through this maze of important information are the *Guide to Genealogical Research in the National Archives* and Michael Tepper's *American Passenger Arrival Records.* Following the wake of these old clippers and steam ships may lead to family records overseas. The genealogical division of your local library may contain numerous volumes that deal with specific countries of origin. These books will outline the best strategies for a particular land should your family-tree climb take you to such faraway places.

7
Old Soldiers Never Die

Often I have opened the folded parchment of old war letters. Like a distant line of skirmishers, the crackle of the yellowed pages seems to erupt with the faint sounds of gunfire. Campfires once bathed these pages and glistened across lines of fresh ink. Some of these old letters echoed the agonies of the killing fields or perhaps a raucous round of laughter from comrades-in-arms. They also captured tender messages from soldiers on the eve of battle—soldiers facing an uncertain charge into a vortex of violence.

One of the intriguing aspects of a family historian's work is to trace military records and reminiscences. Finding soldiers, sailors, or airmen among your kin will connect your family's past with great national events as well as reveal stories of quiet heroism—of duty done, of honor won.

Patriot's Blood

Discovering that you are a son or daughter of the Revolution is an exciting possibility in genealogical research, not because of the prestige of joining a fraternal society so much as the privilege of tracing descent from founding fathers and mothers. To find that an ancestor answered with lead the first British volley at Lexington Green is its own reward. Perhaps when the "sunshine patriots" had gone home, your relative hobbled into winter quarters at Valley

Forge on a line of march that Washington grimly observed could be traced in the scarlet snow left by bare bloodied feet. Maybe he was one of the patriots General Nathaniel Greene had in mind, when the war was being fought as much by grit as by guns, when he said, "We fight, get beat, rise and fight again."

Unfortunately, the records of patriots' service did not survive very well. During the Revolutionary War and for much of a century to follow, military service was conducted by *regulars* and *militia*. Regulars were professional soldiers who made up the core of an army. In the case of the War for Independence, the Continental troops were Washington's regulars. However, militia, or "citizen soldiers," also joined the war effort as part-time soldiers. Records, particularly of militia enlistments and muster, were incomplete even during the war. The service records that have survived are on file in the Revolutionary War Records Collection of the National Archives. For this period, however, pension records, because they are more numerous, are usually more helpful to the genealogist. Early on, the infant states under the Confederation sought to provide pensions for their freedom fighters disabled in the line of service. In 1789 the new federal government assumed these obligations and by 1792 pension applications could be filed directly in federal district courts. Sadly, the wealth of information on these applications was lost in a War Department fire in 1800. Many of the pension records accumulated after 1800 were burned in a second fire in August, 1814. This destruction of veterans' records had an added indignity since the fire was started by marauding British, who torched the capital during the War of 1812.

In the years following, Congress expanded pension eligibility to include, by 1832, all who had served as much as six months, or their widows. Unfortunately, by this late date, more than fifty years after Yorktown, many veterans were not around to collect their pension nor, more importantly for family historians, to leave their names on the Revolutionary roster for their posterity.

This scenario is not provided to discourage searching but rather to help inform. Wide gaps do exist in extant records, but if you have ancestors of the appropriate age during the war years, then it is well worth searching all available records. Your search should include using the invaluable *Index of Revolutionary War Pension Applications in the National Archives* compiled by the National Genealogical Society, or by making a direct research request to the National Archives. Research can be done through the mail by using the NATF Form 80 (see Figure 7-1). The NATF Form 80 is the standard application for all federally housed military archives from the Revolution to World War I. The forms may be obtained free of charge by writing to the National Archives and Records Administration, Reference Service Branch NNRG, Washington, DC 20408.

A few weeks after returning the completed forms, you will be notified whether records are on file relevant to your inquiry. If records are available, then will you be billed (usually $5) for copies of those records.

In addition a number of state and local histories have lists of soldiers and sailors who served the patriots' cause. These volumes may be obtained through the genealogical division of your library or by contacting a local chapter of the Daughters of the American Revolution.

Blue and Gray

Tens of millions of Americans can trace lineal or lateral descent from either Johnny Reb or Billy Yank or both. There were about four million men in uniform on both sides during the Civil War (900,000 in the South and 3 million in the North), and far more public and private records have survived the Civil War than earlier American conflicts. The variety of records provides a number of research avenues to

ORDER FOR COPIES OF VETERANS RECORDS

Please see Page 1 of this form for instructions.

Date Received (NNMS)

1. FILE TO BE SEARCHED (Check one box ONLY)

☐ PENSION ☐ BOUNTY-LAND WARRANT APPLICATION (Service before 1856 only) ☐ MILITARY

3. BRANCH OF SERVICE IN WHICH HE SERVED
☐ Army ☐ Navy ☐ Marine Corps

6. IF SERVICE WAS CIVIL WAR
☐ Union ☐ Confederate

REQUIRED MINIMUM IDENTIFICATION OF VETERAN
Items 2, 3, 4, 5 (and 6 when applicable) MUST be completed or your order cannot be serviced.

2. VETERAN (Give last, first and middle names)

4. STATE FROM WHICH HE SERVED

5. WAR IN WHICH, OR DATES BETWEEN WHICH HE SERVED

PLEASE PROVIDE THE FOLLOWING INFORMATION, IF KNOWN

7. UNIT IN WHICH HE SERVED (Name of regiment or number, company etc. name of ship)

8. IF SERVICE WAS ARMY, ARM IN WHICH HE SERVED
☐ Infantry ☐ Cavalry ☐ Artillery If other, specify

9. KIND OF SERVICE
☐ Volunteers ☐ Regulars

10. PENSION/BOUNTY-LAND FILE NO.

11. IF VETERAN LIVED IN A HOME FOR SOLDIERS GIVE LOCATION (City & State)

12. PLACE(S) VETERAN LIVED AFTER SERVICE

13. DATE OF BIRTH

14. PLACE OF BIRTH (City, County, State etc.)

15. DATE OF DEATH

16. PLACE OF DEATH (City, County, State etc.)

17. NAME OF WIDOW OR OTHER CLAIMANT

Do NOT write below — Space is for our reply to you

☐ **YES** We have located the file you requested above. The cost is $5.00 for the record.

We have copied all or part of the file for you. Make your check or money order for $5.00, payable to **NATIONAL ARCHIVES TRUST FUND (NNMS)**. Do NOT send cash. **Return your payment AND this invoice in the enclosed envelope. If the return envelope is missing**, send your payment AND this invoice to: National Archives Trust Fund Board, P.O. Box 100221, Atlanta, GA 30384. We must have this invoice to match your payment with your copies. WE WILL HOLD THESE COPIES AWAITING RECEIPT OF PAYMENT FOR 30 DAYS ONLY, FROM DATE STAMPED BELOW.

☐ **NO** We were unable to locate the file you requested above.

☐ **REQUIRED MINIMUM IDENTIFICATION OF VETERAN WAS NOT PROVIDED.** Please complete items 2 (give full name), 3, 4, 5, and 6, and resubmit your order.

☐ **A SEARCH WAS MADE BUT THE FILE YOU REQUESTED ABOVE WAS NOT FOUND.** When we do not find a record for a veteran, this does not mean that he did not serve. You may be able to obtain information about him from the archives of the State from which he served.

☐ See attached forms, leaflets, or information sheets.

528259

SEARCHER   **DATE**

FILE DESIGNATION

THIS IS YOUR MAILING LABEL. Print your name (Last, First, MI) and address within the block below. PRESS FIRMLY... the information MUST appear on all copies.
NAME (Last, first, middle)
STREET
CITY STATE

NNMS USE ONLY

ORDER FOR COPIES OF VETERANS RECORDS

INSTRUCTIONS FOR COMPLETING THIS FORM

Submit a separate set of forms for each file you request (see Item 1). WE WILL SEARCH ONLY ONE FILE PER FORM. Remove this instruction sheet. Do NOT remove any of the remaining three pages of this form. Items 2-6 MUST be completed or we cannot search for the file. Print your name (last, first middle) and address in the box provided. This is your mailing label; the information MUST appear on all copies. Mail the completed form to:

Military Service Branch (NNRG)
National Archives and Records Administration
7th and Pennsylvania Avenue, NW
Washington, DC 20408

DO NOT FORWARD PAYMENT WHEN SUBMITTING THIS FORM FOR SEARCH. When we search your order, photocopies will be made of records that relate to your request. At that time we will invoice you for the cost of these copies. WE WILL HOLD THESE COPIES AWAITING RECEIPT OF PAYMENT FOR 30 DAYS ONLY. After that time, you must submit another form to obtain photocopies of the file.

USE ONLY NATF FORM 80 TO OBTAIN COPIES OF VETERANS RECORDS. We cannot process requests submitted on reproductions of this form. Write to the address below to obtain additional copies of this form.

DUE TO THE HEAVY VOLUME OF REQUESTS, PLEASE ALLOW A MINIMUM OF 8-10 WEEKS FOR PROCESSING OF YOUR ORDER.

Do NOT use this form to request photocopies of records relating to service in World War I or II, or subsequent service. Write to: National Personnel Records Center (Military Records), NARA, 9700 Page Boulevard, St. Louis, MO 63132.

IMPORTANT INFORMATION ABOUT YOUR ORDER

We can only search for a record based on the information you provide in Blocks 2-17. The success and accuracy of our search is determined by the completeness and accuracy of the information you provide. When you send more than one form at a time, each form is handled separately. Therefore, you may not receive all of your replies at the same time.

Military service records rarely contain family information. Pension application files generally are most useful to those who are doing genealogical research and contain the most complete information regarding a man's military career. We suggest that you first request copies of a man's pension file. You should request copies of a bounty-land warrant file or a military record only when no pension file exists. If the veteran's service was during the Revolutionary War, bounty-land warrant applications have been consolidated with pension application papers. You can obtain both files by requesting the pension file only.

Often there are many files for veterans of the same or nearly the same name. If there are five or fewer files for men with the same name as the individual in whom you are interested, we will examine all the relevant files and compare their contents with the information that you have provided us. If the veteran's identity seems obvious, we will furnish you a copy of the file we think is the correct one.

If there are more than five files, we will not make a file-by-file check to see if the information in the numerous files matches that provided for the veteran in whom you are interested. In such cases, we suggest that you visit the National Archives and examine the various files, or hire a professional researcher to examine the files for you. We do not maintain a list of persons who do research for a fee; however, many researchers advertise their services in genealogical periodicals, usually available in libraries.

When we are unable to provide copies of all documents, because of the size of a pension or bounty-land warrant application file, we will send copies of the documents we think will be most useful to you. You may order copies of all documents in a file by making a specific request. We will notify you of the cost of the copies.

Additional copies of this form and more information about the availability of records pertaining to military service or family histories may be found in our free genealogical information leaflets and forms. These may be requested by writing to:

Reference Service Branch (NNRG)
National Archives and Records Administration
7th and Pennsylvania Avenue, NW
Washington, DC 20408

PLEASE SEE THE REVERSE OF THIS PAGE FOR THE TYPES OF RECORDS THAT CAN BE ORDERED WITH THIS FORM.

INSTRUCTIONS

NATF Form 80 (11-87)

75

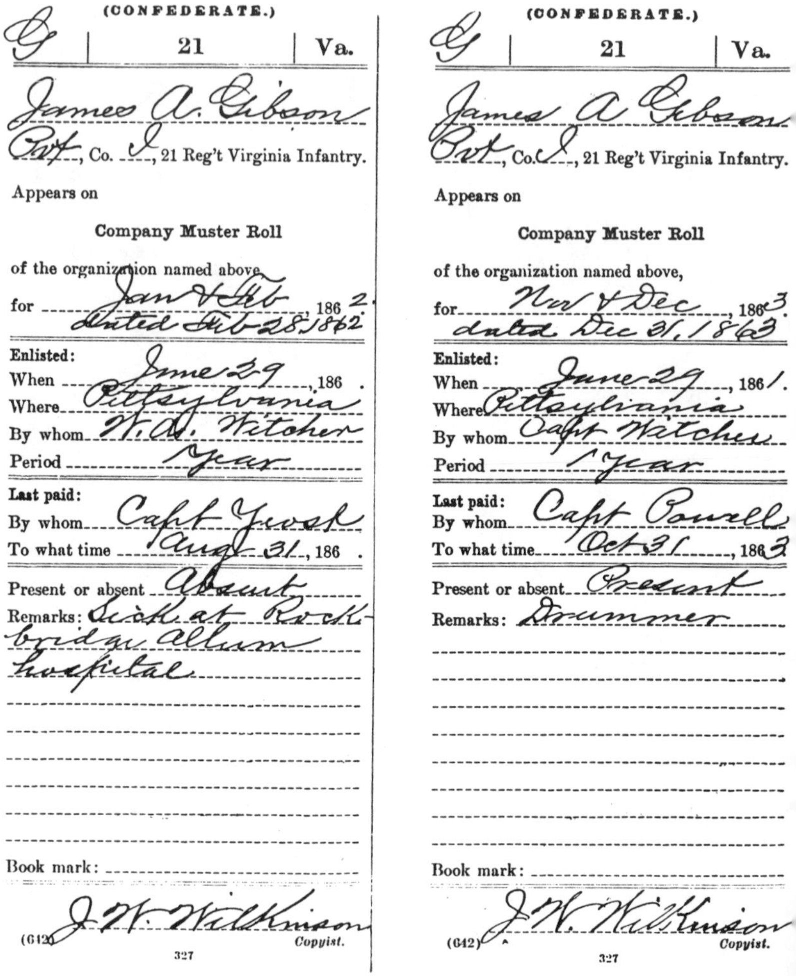

(CONFEDERATE.)

$\mathcal{G}$ | 21 | Va.

James A. Gibson

Pvt., Co. *I*, 21 Reg't Virginia Infantry.

Appears on

Company Muster Roll

of the organization named above,

for *Jan & Feb*, 186 *2*.
dated Feb 28, 1862

Enlisted:
When *June 29*, 186 .
Where *Pittsylvania*
By whom *W. A. Witcher*
Period *1 year*

Last paid:
By whom *Capt Yoost*
To what time *Aug 31*, 186 .

Present or absent *Absent*
Remarks: *Sick at Rock-*
bridge Alum
hospital

Book mark:

(642) *J. W. Wilkinson*

327   *Copyist.*

(CONFEDERATE.)

$\mathcal{G}$ | 21 | Va.

James A Gibson

Pvt., Co. *I*, 21 Reg't Virginia Infantry.

Appears on

Company Muster Roll

of the organization named above,

for *Nov & Dec*, 186 *3*.
dated Dec 31, 1863

Enlisted:
When *June 29*, 186 *1*.
Where *Pittsylvania*
By whom *Capt Witcher*
Period *1 year*

Last paid:
By whom *Capt Powell*
To what time *Oct 31*, 186 *3*.

Present or absent *Present*
Remarks: *Drummer*

Book mark:

(642) *J. W. Wilkinson*

327   *Copyist.*

   Figure 7-2 *Military service record of Pvt. James Gibson,*
21st Virginia Infantry, C.S.A.

Left Card

| 13 Cav. | Ky.

Jesse Sidwell

Priv. Co. 1K, 13 Reg't Kentucky Cavalry.

Age 26 years.

Appears on **Co. Muster-out Roll,** dated

Camp Nelson Ky Jan 10, 1865.

Muster-out to date Jan 10, 1865.

Last paid to Apr 30, 1864.

Clothing account:

Last settled........, 186 ; drawn since $........100

Due soldier $........100 ; due U. S. $........100

Am't for cloth'g in kind or money adv'd $ 94 19/100

Due U. S. for arms, equipments, &c., $ 1 65/100

Bounty paid $........100 ; due $........100

Valuation of horse, $........100

Valuation of horse equipments, $........100

Remarks: *Lee U.S. 1 Carb. box*
& 1 Spurs & Straps 60 ¢ 8/16
pr sentence Regt court Martial
pr orders No 48 dated Hd qrs
B Ky cav. Camp Nelson Dec 23 /64

Book mark:

X *as on Roll.*

O P Webster

(861)   Copyist.

Right Card

N. a 888,198

DROP ORDER AND REPORT.

Department of the Interior,

BUREAU OF PENSIONS,

FINANCE DIVISION.

Washington, D. C., APR 8 1908, 190

Jesse Sidwell
(Pensioner.)

294,291.
(Certificate number.)

INVALID
(Class.)

(Soldier.)

H. 3 Ky. Inf.
(Service.)

U. S. Pension Agent,

Louisville

SIR: You are hereby directed to drop from the roll the name of the above-described pensioner who died *Feby 11*, 1908.

Commissioner.

REPORT.

Commissioner of Pensions.

SIR: The name of the above-described pensioner, who was last paid at $ 24 per month to *Feb 4* 190 , has this day been dropped from the roll of this agency.

U. S. Pension Agent.

April 10, 190 8

Figure 7-3 *Military service and pension records of Pvt. Jesse Sidwell,* **77**
13th Kentucky Cavalry and 3rd Kentucky Infantry, U.S.A.

find out whether any of your ancestors donned Union blue or Confederate gray.

The National Archives is often the place to begin your search for Civil War soldiers in your family. Keep in mind that the War of Brothers touched nearly every family, which means that if you had an ancestor age seventeen through thirty during 1861 to 1865 (although some soldiers were younger and many were older) living in a Union, border, or Confederate state, it would be well worth checking the compiled service records in the National Archives.

As mentioned earlier, the NATF Form 80 is the standard request form for military records from the Revolutionary War to World War I. The minimum information required for initiating a search is the individual's name, home state, branch of service (navy, army, or marines) and whether Union or Confederate. Like most government forms the NATF Form 80 has very narrow parameters. Each request can address only one individual in a specific regiment for a particular kind of record. For example, your ancestor was a sergeant in the 121st New York Regiment who was wounded during the fierce fighting at Bloody Angle during the Wilderness Campaign in May 1864. By December 1864 your sergeant had recovered and was reassigned to the 82nd New York in time to join the siege at Petersburg in the spring of 1865. After the war the veteran applied for a pension which he duly received for his scars. When tracking down all available records on your Union veteran, you would need to designate separate requests for his military records with the 121st New York, his military records with the 82nd New York, his medical records, and his pension records. Court-martial records are filed separately. Requesting records of Confederate veterans is simpler because fewer exist. Only military service records are kept at the National Archives for the gray ranks. If you want more information on a Southern soldier, you must turn to the state he served.

State Records

Appomattox brought peace without peace across Dixie. It was an impoverished land of widows and orphans where the wounds of war were nursed in bitterness until the scars became badges of pride. The disabled Confederates returning home, of course, received no pensions from the federal government. The individual states of the old Confederacy assumed this responsibility many years after the war. The pension applications filed by these graying veterans compose a significant amount of war history and genealogical data. If you suspect you have a Confederate ancestor, you must check beyond the National Archives to the state archives. Appendix A lists the address of each state's archives. If you cannot do the research directly at the state facility, write for information but be sure to provide the research assistant with as much information as possible.

Regimental Histories

Despite the significance and accessibility of the service and pension records in the federal and state archives, the information is sometimes rather sketchy. When you discover a Civil War veteran in your family tree, try to go beyond a mere "name, rank, and serial number" entry. If you know your great-great-grandfather's regiment, track down references to his unit in detailed war histories such as *Battles and Leaders of the Civil War* or the massive 128-volume *Official Records of the Union and Confederate Armies in the War of the Rebellion,* usually referred to as the *OR.*

After the war, hundreds of regimental histories and personal reminiscences from the North and South were published. Even if your veteran ancestor is not specifically mentioned, these histories are immensely valuable. They will, in a sense, permit you to bivouac with his regiment, to join the column of march, and to endure the hardships and heroics of soldiering. For example, my great-great-great-grandfather James Gibson was a private in the 21st Virginia Infantry, one of Stonewall Jackson's crack regiments. After participating in Jackson's brilliant Valley Campaign in May and June 1862, Pvt Gibson's service record at the National Archives states simply *vulnus sclopeticum* at Cedar Run, August 9, 1862. *Vulnus sclopeticum,* or *v.s.,* is an old medical term for a gunshot wound. After consulting Robert Krick's *Stonewall Jackson at Cedar Mountain,* I learned that the 21st Virginia had held the salient against intense artillery fire and some of the fiercest hand-to-hand combat of the war. The unit's stubborn stand took a heavy toll in men killed and wounded but bought Jackson the time he needed to carry the day. Knowing that my forefather had lain wounded on that very battlefield, I was particularly touched to discover the following Confederate diary entry penned in the wake of bloody Cedar Mountain.

If this cruel war lasts seventy-five years, and the Yanks don't kill me before it ends, I hope I will never be compelled to bivouac on another fresh battlefield.

The same silvery moon that flooded the hills of Orange last night hangs again in an unclouded sky and bathes the plains of Culpepper with a sea of mellow light, and the battlefield in a weird silvery glow nearly as light as day. The moonbeams that played last night with velvety fingers, penciling with silvery sheen the silent hieroglyphics of hope that flashed over the cheeks of sleeping soldiers as they dreamed of home and loved ones far away, tonight silently fall and linger on many upturned faces that are cold as marble and wearing the pallid and ghastly hue that can alone be painted by the Angel of Death.

I wonder where that band is that played "Home Sweet Home" last night. I wish it would come right here and play "Come Ye Disconsolate," so as to drown this constant wailing of the wounded.

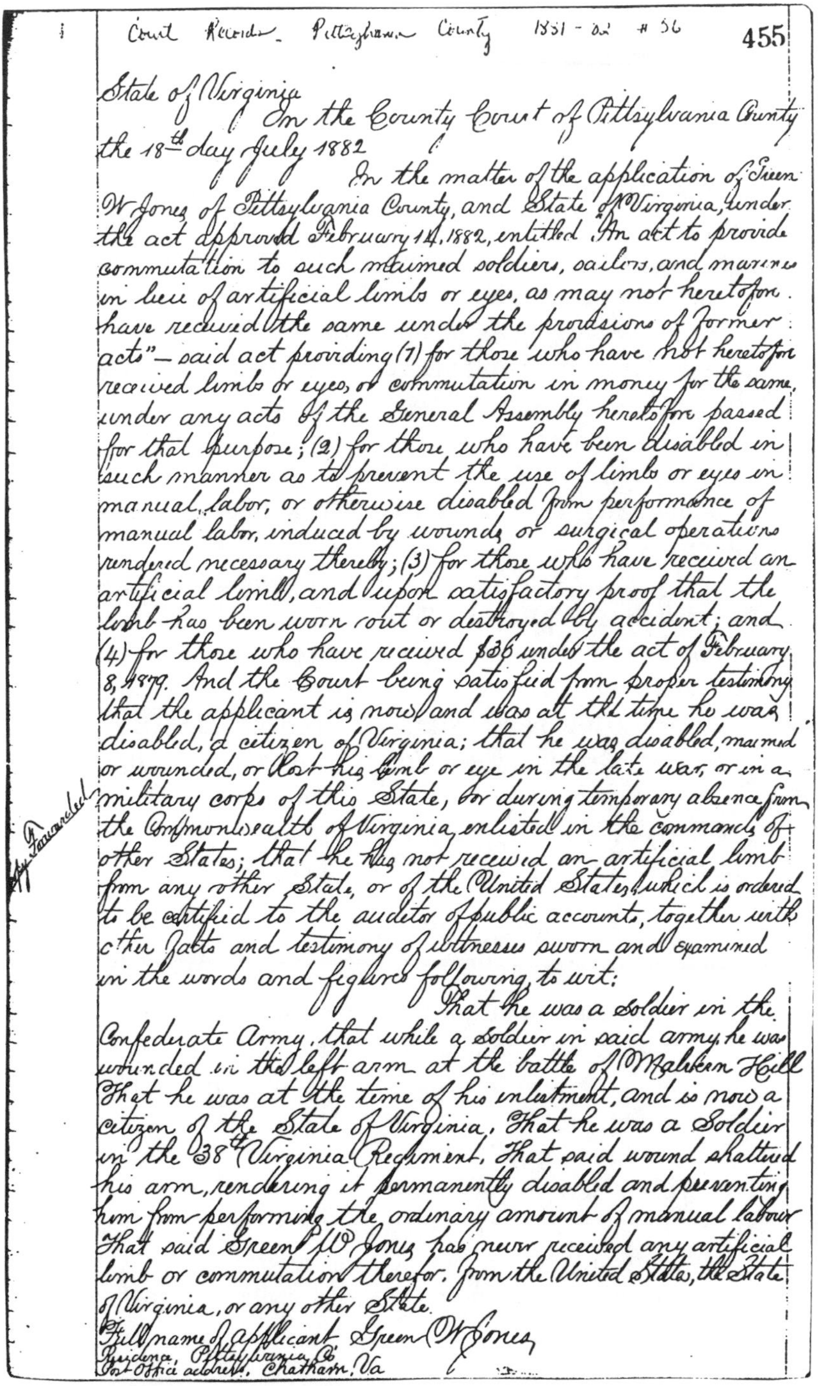

Old Soldiers Never Die

Court Records - Pittsylvania County 1851-82 #56 455

State of Virginia
In the County Court of Pittsylvania County the 18th day July 1882

In the matter of the application of Green W Jones of Pittsylvania County, and State of Virginia, under the act approved February 14, 1882, entitled "An act to provide commutation to such maimed soldiers, sailors, and marines in lieu of artificial limbs or eyes, as may not heretofore have received the same under the provisions of former acts"—said act providing (1) for those who have not heretofore received limbs or eyes, or commutation in money for the same, under any acts of the General Assembly heretofore passed for that purpose; (2) for those who have been disabled in such manner as to prevent the use of limbs or eyes in manual labor, or otherwise disabled from performance of manual labor, induced by wounds or surgical operations rendered necessary thereby; (3) for those who have received an artificial limb, and upon satisfactory proof that the limb has been worn out or destroyed by accident; and (4) for those who have received $36 under the act of February 8, 1879. And the Court being satisfied from proper testimony that the applicant is now and was at the time he was disabled, a citizen of Virginia; that he was disabled, maimed or wounded, or lost his limb or eye in the late war, or in a military corps of this State, or during temporary absence from the Commonwealth of Virginia, enlisted in the commands of other States; that he has not received an artificial limb from any other State, or of the United States, which is ordered to be certified to the auditor of public accounts, together with other facts and testimony of witnesses sworn and examined in the words and figures following, to wit:

That he was a soldier in the Confederate Army, that while a soldier in said army, he was wounded in the left arm at the battle of Malvern Hill. That he was at the time of his enlistment, and is now a citizen of the State of Virginia. That he was a soldier in the 38th Virginia Regiment. That said wound shattered his arm, rendering it permanently disabled and preventing him from performing the ordinary amount of manual labour. That said Green W Jones has never received any artificial limb or commutation therefor, from the United States, the State of Virginia, or any other State.

Full name of applicant Green W Jones,
Residence, Pittsylvania Co
Post Office address, Chatham, Va

Figure 7-4 State pension record for disabled Confederate veteran Green W. Jones 81

If you know your veteran ancestor's regiment, how can you know whether a regimental history was published? The answer will likely be found in *Civil War Books: A Critical Bibliography* by Allan Nevins, James I. Robertson, and Bell Wiley. This two-volume set not only lists most of the Civil War books published from the 1860s to the 1960s but also provides a brief critique which will help you sort the wheat from the chaff. In addition, Charles E. Dornbusch's comprehensive and incomparable *Military Bibliography of the Civil War* (a four-volume set), lists practically every regimental history known as well as journal articles, published speeches, and eulogies. The Nevins, Wiley, and Robertson bibliography and Dornbusch's volumes should be available through interlibrary loan if your local library does not have them.

If your ancestors served in a Virginia unit, you will find the *Virginia Regimental Series* published by H. E. Howard to be helpful. Howard has undertaken the monumental task of publishing separate histories and rosters for each of Virginia's 100 regiments. Narratives such as Bruce Catton's *Mr. Lincoln's Army* and *A Stillness at Appomattox,* or Stephen Sears's *Landscape Turned Red: The Battle of Antietam,* or Bell Wiley's *Shiloh, Bloody April* may also provide colorful insights into your ancestor's war record.

From Belleau Wood to Baghdad

Most of the military service records since World War I are not yet in the public domain. If Grandpa was a doughboy and took up arms against the Huns, his enlistment records may be located in the National Archives but little else. Of course, the millions of service records for World War II and later are also closed.

This lack of public records means that information gathering depends most heavily on personal investigation. Interviews are important, but be particularly sensitive to your interviewee. I have found generally that veterans want to talk about their wartime experiences in inverse proportion to their combat involvement. Sometimes, however, the memories that have been silenced by pain will be triggered, and the stories will come. When this happens, be sure to ask where and when questions and to record the narrative as soon as possible.

Do not overlook more recent military experiences, both wartime and peacetime, in your family history keeping. Military histories of Korea and Vietnam provide campaign details and explain the complexities of Cold War politics, giving you a good background for understanding the era when your father or brother or sister marched on the frontline of world events.

Whether their reminiscences involve slogging through a steaming rice paddy in Vietnam, shivering along Korea's icy Yalu, or readying a front line of bombers with Cold War vigilance at a midwestern air base, they are worth recording. For though the rivers and rice paddies are a world away and the old airstrip is returning to the prairie, the men and women, as freedom fighters, left records that make them worthy heirs of America's first patriots.

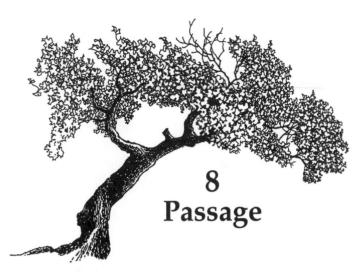

8
Passage

One of the most enjoyable things about climbing a family tree is the climb itself. Alluring clues and intriguing questions will carry you along rutted roads, into sunken cemeteries, through stacks of hide-bound records, and across miles of microfilm. And as you climb, reaching branches of the family that had long ago disappeared into the mists of the past, you will discover that generation upon ever-doubling generation grows into a considerable family of families.

Pilgrim's Progress

One of the mysteries of providence is to see how one family line ends and another survives. Through wars and pestilence and all the vicissitudes of life, one house endures while another falls. One of the rewards of gathering family history is the sense of continuity it provides. However, there are no guarantees on tomorrow. This is why it is most important to be a member of an *everlasting* family—the family of God. Just as membership in your family comes through birth, a place in God's household comes through the new birth. Earthly lineage means nothing, for whether we are descended from princes or paupers, Christ's words to Nicodemus are for everyone: "Ye must be born again." It is complete reliance upon the Saviour, the Lord Jesus, through

His sacrifice at Calvary that brings us into this royal lineage. There is no coat of arms in this family, but there is a robe of righteousness, just as the prophet Isaiah declared: ''I will greatly rejoice in the Lord, my soul shall be joyful in my God; for he hath clothed me with the garments of salvation, he hath covered me with the robe of righteousness'' (61:10).

Therefore, there can be no selfish pride because of membership in God's family, only a thankful heart and a yielded life to the One who ''loved us and gave himself for us.'' I have known descendants of Mayflower Pilgrims who were thoroughly proud of their illustrious lineage without the least knowledge of the personal faith in Christ that motivated those hardy voyagers to come to America. Within a year, most of those Pilgrims had found only an early grave in the wilderness. As believers, to whom death was but the portal to life, even that first grim winter was to be preferred to violating their consciences before God. Their conviction seems strange to modern ears, but it was a day in which people actually died for what they believed.

Despite changing circumstances, their descendants are faced with the same eternal choices about Christ that the Pilgrims once made. Faith is nontransferable; every man and woman must come to terms with whether they will choose Christ and life or self and death. No matter what our spiritual heritage is in this world, the way into God's family is to have a *personal* relationship with Christ. ''As many as received him, to them gave he power to become the sons of God, even to them that believe on his name: Which were born, not of blood, nor of the will of the flesh, nor of the will of man, but of God'' (John 1:12-13).

Distant Music

Time places an impassable barrier behind us. Moments and years and generations are ever slipping into the irretrievable past—this is the challenge that every family historian faces who wants to go beyond merely collecting names and dates. The genealogist must put as much color as possible into the family portrait; otherwise, his chronicle may be little more than a list of begats.

Let the stories, the photographs, the letters, even the lands and houses flesh out your ancestors and help you to get to know them at home, at work, and at play. Of course, time has a way of claiming these *things* as well—pictures fade, epitaphs wash away, houses decay, and plowed fields become parking lots. But even more fragile than papers and places are the people. Take the opportunities that fleeting time permits to hear their stories, record them, and pass them along to the next generation.

From this treasury many wonderful memories can be brought out, dusted off, and enjoyed once again. I began my own family history gathering as a boy walking through red clay fields with my grandfather Keesee, collecting arrowheads and talking—our favorite conversations were always in the past tense. He has long since been laid to rest in the shadow of those fields. Sometimes though, late at night as I work through a family album or an aging sheath of letters, I can almost hear the distant music from his old fiddle. It's the end of a short winter day, firewood crackles by the hearth, supper is over. Mellow lights glow from the windows and across the years as I listen to the fading strains of music. It is a good song; one I must sing to my children.

Glossary

administrator (of an estate)—person empowered to manage or divide the estate of a deceased person

administratrix—a female administrator

alien—foreigner

ante-—Latin prefix, "before," as in *ante-bellum South,* "the South before the war"

attest—to affirm; to certify by signature or oath

B—black; Negro

b—born

banns—public announcement of an intended marriage

bequeath—to grant personal property to a person in a will; noun form: *bequest*

bond—signed and witnessed contract requiring payment of a specified amount of money on or before a given date according to the terms of the agreement

bounty land warrant—the grant of a specific number of acres of public land in compensation for military service

c, ca—from the Latin *circa,* "about, approximately"

census—official enumeration or counting of citizens

co—county or company

codicil—addition to a will

col—"colored;" Negro, black

Confederate—pertaining to the Southern states' government and the citizens of the Confederacy, 1861-65

consort—usually a wife whose husband is living

conveyance—a deed

cousin—often a loose term for a relative descended from a common ancestor, but not a brother or sister

CSA—Confederate States of America

C.V.—Confederate veteran (may appear on tombstones)

d—died

dau—daughter

daughter-in-law—wife of one's son

dea—deacon

decedent—a deceased person

decd—deceased

Declaration of Intention—an alien's sworn statement documenting his desire to become a citizen

deed—transfer of ownership of property

Deo Vindice—Latin, "God defending"; the motto of the Confederacy, often appears on Confederate veteran burial markers

devise—a gift of real property; differs from a bequest, which involves personal property

devisee—one to whom property is given in a will

devisor—one who gives property in a will

dissenter—one who did not belong to the established church, especially the Anglican Church during the colonial period

dower—a wife's legal entitlement to the estate of her husband allotted to her after his death for her lifetime

D.V.—Latin *deo volente*, "if God wills"; appears in correspondence and wills

emigrant—one leaving a country and moving to another

enumeration—listing or counting, such as a census

esquire—in England, a designation of genteel social rank just below a knight; in America, loosely applied to professionals such as doctors, lawyers, and clergymen

estate—all property and debts belonging to a person

etc.—Latin *et cetera,* "and other things"

et al.—Latin *et alii,* "and others"

et uxor—Latin, "and his wife;" appears in probate abstracts, often abreviated *et ux*

executor—one appointed in a will to carry out provisions

f—female

father-in-law—father of one's spouse

fee or fee simple—the clear and complete right to devise or convey real property

fiduciary—a person in a legal position of trust over another's estates, such as an executor or guardian

fmc—free man of color

fwc—free woman of color

G.A.R.—Grand Army of the Republic; Union veterans' organization

genealogy—study of family history and descent

given name—name given to a person at birth or baptism, one's first and middle names

govt—government

great-aunt—sister of one's grandparent

great-uncle—brother of one's grandparent

guardian—person appointed to care for and manage property of a minor orphan or an adult incapable of managing his own affairs

half-brother (half-sister)—the relationship of two people who have only one parent in common

heirs—those entitled by law or by the terms of a will to inherit property

Homestead Act—Congressional act of 1862 granting a head of a household title to 160 acres of public land after clearing and improving it for 5 years

ibid.—Latin *ibidem*, "in the same place;" a reference footnote used to mean the same work previously cited

illegitimate—born to a mother who was not married to the child's father

immigrant—one moving into a country from another

indentured servant—a person who bound himself into service of another person for a specified number of years, usually in exchange for passage to this country

instant—(calendar) of the current month

intestate—one who dies without a will, as in *He died intestate.*

IOOF—Independent Order of Odd Fellows, fraternal organization

issue—offspring; children

JP—Justice of the Peace

late—recently deceased; now deceased

LDS—The Church of Jesus Christ of Latter-Day Saints, the Mormons

legacy—property left to a devisee in a will

lineage—ancestry; direct descent from a specific ancestor; adjective form: *lineal*

lodge—chapter or meeting hall of a fraternal organization

LS—Latin *locus sigilli;* on documents, the place where a man's seal is placed

m—male

m—married

m1—married first

m2—married second

maternal—related through one's mother. The maternal grandmother is the mother's mother.

MG— Minister of the Gospel

microfiche—sheet of microfilm usually measuring 4" × 6" with greatly reduced images of pages of documents

microfilm—reproduction of documents on film at reduced size

migrate—to move from one country or region to another

militia—state citizens who are not part of the national military forces but who can be called into military service in an emergency; a citizen army apart from the regular military forces

minor—one who is under legal age; not yet a legal adult

moiety—a probate term for half

mortality—death; death rate

mortality schedules—enumeration of persons who died during the year prior to June 1 of 1850, 1860, 1870, and 1880 in each state in the United States, conducted by the Bureau of the Census

mother-in-law—mother of one's spouse

Mu—Mulatto, person with one Caucasian parent and one Negro parent

namesake—person named after another person

nd—no date given

necrology—record of persons who have died recently

née—(pronounced [nā], French feminine of "to be born") used to identify a woman's maiden name: *Mrs. Melba Clark, née Vowell*

nephew—son of one's brother or sister

niece—daughter of one's brother or sister

nm—never married

np—no page given or no publisher given

NS—New Style, referring to the Gregorian calendar

obit—Latin, "he died"

OM—Ordained Minister

OS—Old Style, referring to the Julian calendar

O.S.P.—Latin *obit since prole,* "died without issue"

patent—individual land grant from a government

paternal—related through one's father. The paternal grandmother is the father's mother.

pedigree—family tree; ancestry

pension—money paid regularly to an individual, especially by a government as reward for military service during wartime or upon retirement from government service

pensioner—one who receives a pension

poll—list or record of person, especially for taxing or voting

post-—Latin prefix, "after," as in *post–World War II* or *postwar*

posterity—descendants; those who come after

pp—pages

pre-—Latin prefix, "before," as in *pre–World War I* or *prewar*

probate—the process of validating a will or the courts that deal with wills and the administration of estates

progenitor—a direct ancestor

proximo—in the following month, in the month after the present one

public domain—land owned by the government

relict—widow

R.I.P.—Latin *requiescut in pace,* "may he, or she, rest in peace"

sibling—person having one or both parents in common with another; a brother or sister

sic—Latin meaning "thus"; copied exactly as the original reads; often suggests a mistake in the original

son-in-law—husband of one's daughter

spouse—husband or wife

statute—law

step-brother (step-sister)—child of one's step-father or step-mother

step-child—child of one's husband or wife from a previous marriage

step-father—husband of one's mother by a later marriage

step-mother—wife of one's father by a later marriage

surname—family name or last name

territory—a region of the United States prior to statehood, having its own legislature and governor, such as the *Dakota Territory*

testator—person who makes a valid will before his death

tithable—taxable

tithe—formerly, money due as a tax for support of the clergy or church

Tory—Loyalist; a British sympathizer during the American Revolution

township—division of U. S. public land that contained 36 sections, or 36 square miles; a subdivision of the county in many Northeastern and Midwestern states of the United States

U.C.V.—United Confederate Veterans

ultimo—last, as in the month before this one

unm—unmarried

VDM—Latin *Verbi Domini Ministerium,* "minister of the Word of God"

vital records—records of birth, death, marriage, and divorce

viz—from the Latin *videlicet,* "namely"

w—white; Caucasian

(w) or wit—witness

will—document declaring how a person wants his property divided after his death

witness—one who is present at a legal transaction, such as the signing of a will or bond, who can testify that it actually took place

Appendix A

State Archives

Alabama: State of Alabama
Department of Archives and History
624 Washington Avenue
Montgomery, AL 36130

Alaska: Alaska Historical Library
Alaska Division of State Libraries
State Office Building
Juneau, AK 99801

Arizona: Department of Library and Archives
Capitol Building, Third Floor
Phoenix, AZ 85007

Arkansas: Arkansas History Commission
One Capitol Mall
Little Rock, AR 72201

California: California State Archives
1020 O Street, Room 130
Sacramento, CA 95814

Colorado: Division of State Archives
and Public Records
1313 Sherman Street
Denver, CO 80203

Connecticut: Connecticut State Library
231 Capitol Avenue
Hartford, CT 06115

Delaware: Bureau of Archives-Modern Records
Hall of Records
Dover, DE 19901

Florida: Florida State Archives
Department of State
R. A. Gray Building
Tallahassee, FL 32301

Georgia: Georgia Department of Archives
and History
330 Capitol Avenue, SW
Atlanta, GA 30334

Hawaii: Public Archives Library
Iolani Palace Grounds
Honolulu, HI 96813

Idaho: Idaho State Archives
325 West State Street
Boise, ID 83702

Illinois: The Director
Archives-Records Management Division
Office of the Secretary of State
Springfield, IL 62756

Indiana: Archives and Records
Management Division
140 North Senate Avenue
Indianapolis, IN 46204

Iowa: State Historical Society of Iowa
East 12th and Grand Avenue
Des Moines, IA 50319

Kansas: Kansas State Historical Society
Department of Archives
Center for Historical Research
120 West 10th Street
Topeka, KS 66612

*Kentucky: Kentucky Historical Society
Old State House
P. O. Box H
Frankfort, KY 40601

Louisiana: State of Louisiana
Secretary of State
Division of Archives, Records Management,
and History
P. O. Box 94125
Baton Rouge, LA 70804-9125

Maine: State of Maine
Maine State Archives
L-M-A Building
State House Station 84
Augusta, ME 04333

Maryland: Maryland State Archives
350 Rowe Boulevard
Annapolis, MD 21401

Massachusetts: The Commonwealth of Massachusetts
The Adjutant General's Office
Military Records Section, Room 1000
100 Cambridge Street
Boston, MA 02202

Michigan: Michigan Department of State
Bureau of History
State Archives
3405 North Logan Street
Lansing, MI 48918

Minnesota: Division of Library and Archives
Minnesota Historical Society
1500 Mississippi Street
St. Paul, MN 55101

Mississippi: Archives and Library Division
Department of Archives and History
P. O. Box 571
Jackson, MS 39205

Missouri: Adjutant General's Office
1717 Industrial Drive
Jefferson City, MO 65101

Montana: Montana State Library
930 East Lyndale Avenue
Helena, MT 59601

Nebraska: Nebraska State Historical Society Library
1500 R Street
Lincoln, NE 68508

Nevada: Nevada State Library and Archives
Division of Archives and Records
101 South Fall Street
Carson City, NV 89710

New Hampshire: Division of Records and Archives
71 South Fruit Street
Concord, NH 03301

New Jersey: Department of State
Division of Archives and Records Manager
Archives Section
185 West State Street, CN 307
Trenton, NJ 08625

New Mexico: State Records Center and Archives
404 Montezuma
Santa Fe, NM 87503

New York: New York State Archives
Room 11D40
Cultural Education Center
Empire State Plaza
Albany, NY 12230

North Carolina: Division of Archives and History
Department of Cultural Resources
109 E. Jones Street
Raleigh, NC 27611

North Dakota: North Dakota State Historical Society
Liberty Memorial Building
State Capitol Grounds
Bismarck, ND 58501

*Ohio: Ohio State Archives Library
1985 Velma Avenue
Columbus, OH 43211

Oklahoma: Division of Library Resources
Oklahoma Historical Society
Historical Building
Oklahoma City, OK 73105

Oregon: Oregon State Archives
Oregon State Library
State Library Building
Salem, OR 97310

Pennsylvania: Director
Pennsylvania Historical and Museum
   Commission
Archives Building
Box 1026
Harrisburg, PA 17108-1026

Rhode Island: Rhode Island State Archives
314 State House
Providence, RI 02903

South Carolina: South Carolina Department
   of Archives and History
P. O. Box 11
669 Capitol Station
Columbia, SC 29211

South Dakota: Historical Resources Center
Memorial Building
Pierre, SD 57501

Tennessee: Public Service Station
Tennessee State Library and Archives
403 7th Avenue North
Nashville, TN 37219-5041

Texas: Texas State Library
Archives Division
P. O. Box 12927
Austin, TX 78711

Utah: State Archives
State Capitol Building
Salt Lake City, UT 84114

Vermont: State Veterans Affairs
State Office Building
Montpelier, VT 05602

Virginia: Archives Division
Virginia State Library
11th and Capitol Streets
Richmond, VA 23219

Washington: Division of Archives and
Records Management
12th and Washington Streets
Olympia, WA 98501

West Virginia: West Virginia Department of Culture
and History
Division of Archives and History
The Cultural Center
Capitol Complex
Charleston, WV 25305

Wisconsin: Reference Archivist
The State Historical Society
of Wisconsin
816 State Street
Madison, WI 53706

Wyoming: Wyoming State Archives
and Historical Department
State Office Building
Cheyenne, WY 82001

*No research conducted by mail.

Appendix B

Federal Records Centers—
Regional Branches of the National Archives

Atlanta Federal Archives and Records Center
1557 St. Joseph Avenue
East Point, GA 30344
for Alabama, Georgia, Florida, Kentucky, Mississippi,
North Carolina, South Carolina, and Tennessee

Boston Federal Archives and Records Center
380 Trapelo Road
Waltham, MA 02154
for Connecticut, Maine, Massachusetts, New Hampshire,
Rhode Island, and Vermont

Chicago Federal Archives and Records Center
7358 South Pulaski Road
Chicago, IL 60629
for Illinois, Indiana, Michigan, Minnesota, Ohio, and
Wisconsin.

Denver Federal Archives and Records Center
Building 48, Denver Federal Center
Denver, CO 80225
for Colorado, Montana, North Dakota, South Dakota,
Utah, and Wyoming

Fort Worth Federal Archives and Records Center
4900 Hemphill Street
Fort Worth, TX 76115
for Arkansas, Louisiana, New Mexico, Oklahoma, and
Texas. Includes special collections of Indian records.

Kansas City Federal Archives and Records Center
2306 East Bannister Road
Kansas City, MI 64131
for Iowa, Kansas, Missouri, and Nebraska

Los Angeles Federal Archives and Records Center
24000 Avila Road
Laguna Niguel, CA 92677
for Arizona, Southern California, and Clark County, Nevada

New York Federal Archives and Records Center
Building 22—MOT Bayonne
Bayonne, New Jersey 07002
for New Jersey, New York, Puerto Rico, and Virgin Islands

Philadelphia Federal Archives and Records Center
5000 Wissahickon Avenue
Philadelphia, PA 19144
for Delaware, Pennsylvania, District of Columbia, Maryland, Virginia, and West Virginia

San Francisco Federal Archives and Records Center
1000 Commodore Drive
San Bruno, CA 94066
for Northern California, Hawaii, Nevada (except Clark County), and territories in the Pacific. Includes special material pertaining to American Samoa.

Seattle Federal Archives and Records Center
6125 Sand Point Way NE
Seattle, WA 98115
for Alaska, Idaho, Oregon, and Washington

State	Became a territory	Became a state	1st available census	Status Comments	Missing Censuses 1790	1800	1810	1820	1830	1840	1850	1860	1870
Alabama	1817	1819	1830	Before 1817 Ala. formed the eastern half of the Miss. Terr.			All (as part of the Miss. Terr.)	All (Census of some counties is in *Alabama Historical Quarterly* - Fall 1944, Vol. 6.)					
Alaska	1912	1959	1900										
Arizona	1863	1912	1870 (1850 and 1860 are in New Mexico)	Ariz. was in N.M. Terr. 1850-63.									
Arkansas	1819	1836	1830	Ark. was part of the Mo. Terr. 1812-19. The Ark. Terr. included the Indian lands in Okla.				All				Little River County	
California		1850	1850	Owned by Mexico 1822-1848							San Francisco, Santa Clara, and Contra Costa cos.		

Climbing Your Family Tree

FEDERAL CENSUS DATA

State	Became a territory	Became a state	1st available census	Status Comments	Missing Censuses								
					1790	1800	1810	1820	1830	1840	1850	1860	1870
Colorado	1861	1876	1870 1860 Census of Arapahoe Co. in Kan. Territory	Colo. Territory was a combination of about 50 million acres previously assigned to Utah and Kansas, and about 10 million from the N. M. Terr.									
Connecticut		1788	1790	One of the original 13 states									
Delaware		1787	1800		(All reconstructed)								
District of Columbia	1790	Became t govt. in 1	1800 Part of 1 Montgom Prince G counties			Incomplete	All (includin Alexandria now in Va.)						

108

State	Became a territory	Became a state	1st available census	Status Comments	Missing Censuses 1790	1800	1810	1820	1830	1840	1850	1860	1870
Florida	1822	1845	1830	Fla. Territory originally included parts of southern Miss. and Ala.								Hernando County	
Georgia		1788	1820	One of the original 13 states	All (reconstructed)	All except Oglethorpe County	All	Franklin, Rabun, and Twiggs cos.					
Hawaii	1900	1959	1900	Ceded itself to U.S. in 1898									
Idaho	1863	1890	1870 (Part in Utah census)	Part of the Oregon Terr., 1848-53; Wash. Terr., 1853-63; became Idaho Terr. in 1863									Kootenai County
Illinois	1809	1818	1820	Original Ill. Terr. included area of present Wisc. and eastern Minn.		All (as part of the Ind. Terr.)	All except Randolph County						

FEDERAL CENSUS DATA

State	Became a territory	Became a state	1st available census	Status Comments	Missing Censuses								
					1790	1800	1810	1820	1830	1840	1850	1860	1870
Indiana	1800	1816	1820	Ind. Territory included Ill., Wisc., western Mich., & eastern Minn.		All	All	Daviess County	*				
Iowa	1838	1846	1840	Iowa was in Mo. Terr. 1812-21; an unorganized territory 1821-34; Mich. Terr. 1834-36; Wisc. Terr. 1836-38.									
Kansas	1854	1861	1860	Kansas was in Mo. Terr. 1812-21; unorganized territory (Indian) 1821-54.									Arapahoe County
Kentucky		1792	1810	Originally Ky. was considered part of Augusta Co., Va., then part of Virginia Co., Va., then later Fincastle Co., Va. During early settlement, it was called Kentucky Co., Va. (c. 1775-76). In 1776 it was divided into 3 counties—Fayette, Jefferson, and Lincoln. It was further divided into 9 counties in 1790.	All (Tax lists have been substituted.)	All (Tax lists have been substituted.)							

* Wabash County, Indiana, for 1830 was originally reported missing. However, the county was not created until 1832 (from Cass and Grant counties).

State	Became a territory	Became a state	1st available census	Status Comments	1790	1800	1810	1820	1830	1840	1850	1860	1870
Louisiana	1805	1812	1810	Southern part of Lousiana Purchase became Orleans Terr. in 1804.			St. Landry and W. Baton Rouge p'sh and some areas no longer in state					Bienville Parish	
Maine		1820	1790 (in Mass.)	Annexed in 1693 as York(shire) Co., Mass., and remained part of Mass. until 1820, when Maine became a separate state		Part of York Co.							
Maryland		1788	1790	One of the original 13 states	Allegany, Calvert, and Somerset counties	All of Baltimore Co. except the City of Baltimore			Montgomery, Prince George's, St. Mary's, Queen Anne's, and Somerset counties				
Massachusetts		1788	1790	One of the original 13 states; included Maine until 1820		Part of Suffolk County							

Climbing Your Family Tree

FEDERAL CENSUS DATA

State	Became a territory	Became a state	1st available census	Status Comments	1790	1800	1810	1820	1830	1840	1850	1860	1870
Michigan	1805	1837	1820	Jurisdiction extended west to the Miss. River, including Wisc. and eastern Minn. (1818-36)									
Minnesota	1849	1858	1850 (There was also a special enumeration in 1857.)	The Minn. Terr. (1849) extended western to the Mo. River, including much of what later became the Dakota Territory.									All originals missing except the counties alphabetically from Stearns to Wright. (State Hist. Soc. and Nat'l Archives have copies of missing schedules.)
Mississippi	1798	1817	1820	Originally claimed by Ga. Remained loyal to the Crown during Revolutionary War but was taken over by Spain 1789-91. Held by Spain until 1798. All of the state south of 31st parallel was in Spanish west Fla. until		All	All (including Alabama)		Pike County				Hancock, Sunflower, and Washington counties

State	Became a territory	Became a state	1st available census	Status Comments	Missing Censuses 1790	1800	1810	1820	1830	1840	1850	1860	1870
Missouri	1812	1821	1830	Northern part of the La. Prchs. was made Mo. Terr. in 1812. Originally this territory included Ark., Iowa, Kan., Neb., and Okla.			All (in La. Terr.)	All					
Montana	1864	1889	1860 (in Neb. Terr. and Wash. Terr.)	In La. Terr. 1805-12; Mo. Terr. 1812-54; Neb. Terr. 1854-61; Dakota Terr. 1861-64.									
Nebraska	1854	1864	1860	Part of Mo. Terr. 1812-20 (no settlers until 1823), unorganized territory 1820-34. When Neb. Terr. was created, it included parts of Colo., Mont., Wyo., and North and South Dakota Terr. Area was reduced to present size of state in 1861 with creation of Colorado and Dakota Terr.									
Nevada	1861	1864	1860 (in Utah Terr.)	From 1850 to 1861 it was part of Utah Terr., except southern tip of state which was in N. M. Terr. 1850-63, before Ariz. Terr. was organized.									

FEDERAL CENSUS DATA

State	Became a territory	Became a state	1st available census	Status Comments	Missing Censuses								
					1790	1800	1810	1820	1830	1840	1850	1860	1870
New Hampshire		1788	1790	One of the original 13 states		Parts of Rockingham and Strafford counties		Grafton Co.; parts of Rockingham and Strafford counties					
New Jersey		1787	1830	One of the original 13 states	All	All	All	All					
New Mexico	1850	1912	1850	Territory originally included Ariz. and part of Colorado.									
New York		1788	1790	One of the original 13 states			Courtland County						
North Carolina		1789	1790	One of the original 13 states; included Tennessee until 1796	Caswell, Granville, and Orange counties		Craven, Green, New Hanover, and Wake counties	Currituck, Franklin, Martin, Montgomery, Randolph, and Wake counties					

State	Became a territory	Became a state	1st available census	Status Comments	Missing Censuses 1790	1800	1810	1820	1830	1840	1850	1860	1870
North Dakota	1861	1889	1860 (as the Dakota Terr.)	Unorganized part of Minn. Terr. until 1859 when Minn. was cut to its present boundaries. As Dakota Terr. was organized in 1861 it included both Dakotas and most of Wyo. and Mont. In 1864 Wyo. and Mont. separated to form Mont. Terr. In 1889 the Dakotas were divided.									
Ohio	1788	1803	1820	Originally part of the N.W. Terr. (1787)			All	All	Franklin and Wood counties				
Oklahoma	1890	1907	1890 (partial)	Okla. became part of the Ark. Terr. in 1819. Indian tribes ceded the western portion of their domain to the U.S. in 1866. Land was opened for white settlement in 1889.									
Oregon	1848	1859	1850	Oregon Terr. embraced all of Wash. and Idaho, British Columbia to 54° 40', and Mont. and Wyo. west of the continental divide until cut to present size to become a state.									

Climbing Your Family Tree

FEDERAL CENSUS DATA

State	Became a territory	Became a state	1st available census	Status Comments	Missing Censuses 1790	1800	1810	1820	1830	1840	1850	1860	1870
Pennsylvania		1787	1790	One of the original 13 states	Part of Westmoreland County	Parts of Bedford, Cumberland, and Philadelphia counties							
Rhode Island		1790	1790	One of the original 13 states									
South Carolina		1788	1790	One of the original 13 states	Richland County								
South Dakota	1861	1889	1860 (as the Dakota Terr.)	When the Dak. Terr. was created in 1861, it included both Dakotas and most of Mont. and Wyo. In 1864 Mont. and Wyo. separated to form the Mont. Terr., and in 1889 the Dakotas were divided into two states.									

State	Became a territory	Became a state	1st available census	Status Comments	Missing Censuses 1790	1800	1810	1820	1830	1840	1850	1860	1870
Tennessee		1796	1820 (one county in 1810)	Tenn. was originally a part of N.C. In the early settlement period it was called Washington Co., N.C.	All (part reconstructed from tax lists)		All missing except Rutherford County. Grainger County published.	Anderson, Bledsoe, Blount, Campbell, Carter, Claiborne, Cocke, Grainger, Greene, Hamilton, Hawkins, Jefferson, Knox, McMinn, Marion, Monroe, Morgan, Rhea, Roane, Sevier, Sullivan, and Washington counties					
Texas		1845	1850	Texas belonged to Mexico until an independent republic was set up in 1836 by the settlers.								Blanco, Coleman, Concho, Duval, Edwards, Hardeman, Kimble, Knox, LaSalle, McCulloch, McCullen, Tarrant, Taylor, Wichita, Wilbarger, and Wilson counties.	Archer, Baylor, Concho, Edwards, Hardeman, Knox, Taylor, Wichita, and Wilbarger counties

FEDERAL CENSUS DATA

State	Became a territory	Became a state	1st available census	Status Comments	Missing Censuses								
					1790	1800	1810	1820	1830	1840	1850	1860	1870
Utah	1850	1896	1850	Original territory included all of Nevada except southern tip. It also included western Colo. and southwest Wyo. (as far north as the present Utah-Idaho border).									
Vermont		1791	1790		All (Tax lists have been substituted.)								
Virginia		1788	1810	One of the original 13 states; included W.Va. until 1863; Ky. until 1792. Alexandria Co. was in the Dist. of Col. in the censuses of 1820, 1830, and 1840.	All	Alexandria,Cabell, Grayson, Greenbrier, Halifax, Hardy, James City, King Wm., Lee, Louisa, Mecklenburg, Nansemond, Northampton, Orange, Patrick, Pittsylvania, Russell, and Tazewell counties							

State	Became a territory	Became a state	1st available census	Status Comments	Missing Censuses								
					1790	1800	1810	1820	1830	1840	1850	1860	1870
Washington	1853	1889	1860	In Oregon Terr. 1848-53									
West Virginia		1863	1810 (in Va.)	Separated itself from Va. during the Civil War	All (part of Va.)	All (part of Va.)	Cabell, Greenbrier, and Hardy counties (in Va.)						
Wisconsin	1836	1848	1820 (in Mich. Terr.)	Originally the Wisconsin Terr. extended west as far as Mo. River and included what later became the Minn. Terr. and much of the Dakota Terr.		All (as part of Indiana Terr.)	All (as part of Illinois Terr.)						
Wyoming	1868	1890	1860 (in Neb. Terr.)	Wyoming was in Neb. Terr. 1854-61; Dakota Terr. 1861-64; Mont. Terr. 1864-68. The extreme western part was in the Ore. Terr. 1848-53; Wash. Terr. 1853-63; Idaho Terr. 1863-68; and the southwest corner was in Utah Terr. 1850-68.									

Adapted from *The Researcher's Guide to American Genealogy* by Val D. Greenwood